# Contents

# Carry On

Find the answers to these problems, and then write the answers in order from smallest to largest at the bottom of the page.

**Skills:**

Computation of Multiple-Digit Whole Numbers

Arranging Numbers in Order

1. 8,376
   + 6,825
   = 15,201

2. 5,268
   + 9,760
   = 15,028

3. 1,425
   + 5,285
   = 6,710

4. 8,605
   + 3,497
   = 12,102

5. 4,625
   − 1,709
   = 2,916

6. 5,215
   − 2,166
   = 3,049

7. 6,850
   − 2,279
   = 4,571

8. 9,605
   − 4,238
   = 5,367

9. 839
   × 72
   1678
   58730
   60,408

10. 456
    × 18
    3648
    4560
    8,208

11. 1,823
    × 56
    10928
    91150
    102,088

12. 7,069
    × 67
    49483
    424140
    473,623

13. 49)2,450  50

14. 33)7,095  215

15. 71)3,692  52

16. 62)26,040  420

Deep Blue Sea

Complete each multiplication problem. Write the corresponding letter on the line above the answer. The letters will spell out the answer to this riddle.

## Why are fish so smart?

**Deep Blue Sea**

**A**  24 × 73 = _____

**B**  81 × 94 = _____

**C**  32 × 95 = _____

**E**  38 × 72 = _____

**H**  40 × 102 = _____

**I**  804 × 18 = _____

**L**  412 × 21 = _____

**N**  329 × 89 = _____

**O**  104 × 53 = _5,512_

**S**  210 × 42 = _____

**T**  2,952 × 15 = _____

**U**  4,201 × 20 = _____

**V**  285 × 21 = _____

**Y**  235 × 28 = _____

---

| ___ | ___ | ___ | ___ | ___ | ___ | ___ |
|---|---|---|---|---|---|---|
| 7,614 | 2,736 | 3,040 | 1,752 | 84,020 | 8,820 | 2,736 |

| ___ | ___ | ___ | ___ |
|---|---|---|---|
| 44,280 | 4,080 | 2,736 | 6,580 |

| ___ | ___ | ___ | ___ | | ___ | ___ |
|---|---|---|---|---|---|---|
| 8,652 | 14,472 | 5,985 | 2,736 | | 14,472 | 29,281 |

| ___ | ___ | ___ | O | O | ___ | ___ |
|---|---|---|---|---|---|---|
| 8,820 | 3,040 | 4,080 | 5,512 | 5,512 | 8,652 | 8,820 |

# A Riddle

To answer the riddle, draw a straight line between each division problem on the left and its answer on the right. Each line will go through at least one number. Write the corresponding letter in the box above each number. The letters will spell out the solution to the riddle.

**Skills:**

Dividing Whole Numbers with up to Two-Digit Divisors

## How do you know a shark has been swimming in your bathtub?

| | | |
|---|---|---|
| **A** | 280 ÷ 28 | • |
| **E** | 210 ÷ 15 | • |
| **H** | 1,342 ÷ 61 | • |
| **I** | 238 ÷ 14 | • |
| **K** | 210 ÷ 6 | • |
| **M** | 408 ÷ 51 | • |
| **N** | 45 ÷ 15 | • |
| **O** | 912 ÷ 48 | • |
| **P** | 99 ÷ 9 | • |
| **R** | 294 ÷ 42 | • |
| **S** | 552 ÷ 46 | • |
| **T** | 245 ÷ 49 | • |

• 3
• 5
2
• 7
• 8
• 10
• 11
• 12
• 14
• 17
• 19
• 22
• 35

9   11   12   13   7   14   16   5   10   15   1   3   8   6

| | 1 | 10 | 10 | 2 | 16 |
|---|---|---|---|---|---|

| | A | | | | | 7 | 12 |
|---|---|---|---|---|---|---|---|
| 13 | 9 | 15 | 5 | 3 | | 7 | 12 |

| | | | | | A | |
|---|---|---|---|---|---|---|
| 8 | 16 | 11 | 14 | 10 | 9 | 6 |

Deep Blue Sea

**Skills:**

Determining
Place Value

Find the place value of the digit **5** in each number. Then write the corresponding letter above the number. The letters will spell out a tongue twister. Try to say it fast three times.

| | | | |
|---|---|---|---|
| ones | **M** | hundred thousands | **P** |
| tens | **C** | millions | **R** |
| hundreds | **I** | ten millions | **S** |
| thousands | **K** | hundred millions | **X** |
| ten thousands | **H** | | |

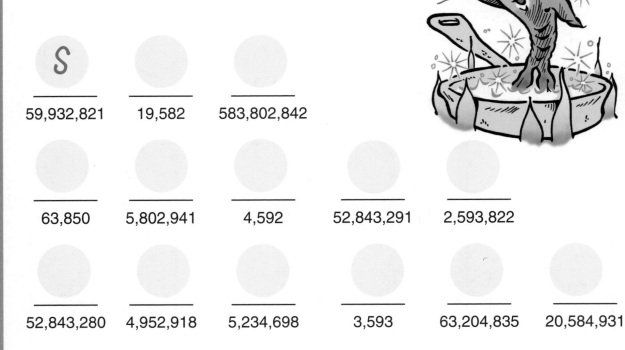

$\mathcal{S}$

| | | |
|---|---|---|
| _____ | _____ | _____ |
| 59,932,821 | 19,582 | 583,802,842 |

| | | | | |
|---|---|---|---|---|
| _____ | _____ | _____ | _____ | _____ |
| 63,850 | 5,802,941 | 4,592 | 52,843,291 | 2,593,822 |

| | | | | | |
|---|---|---|---|---|---|
| _____ | _____ | _____ | _____ | _____ | _____ |
| 52,843,280 | 4,952,918 | 5,234,698 | 3,593 | 63,204,835 | 20,584,931 |

# Number Names

## Write these numbers:

**1.** nine thousand, eight hundred seventy-five          _____

**2.** twenty-seven thousand, four hundred nine          _____

**3.** six hundred thirty-five thousand, nine hundred fifty-six          _____

**4.** eight million, six hundred thousand, two hundred twenty-seven

_____

## Write these numbers in words:

**5.** 4,689

_____ four thousand-six-hundred eighty-nine

**6.** 27,205

_____

**7.** 643,817

_____

_____

**8.** 1,309,762

_____

_____

## Write these numbers in expanded form:

**9.** 2,683          2,000 + 600 + 80 + 3

**10.** 16,520          _____

**11.** 587,400          _____

**12.** 4,305,891          _____

Deep Blue Sea

# Function Tables

Complete each of the following function tables using the given rule:

**1.**

| Rule = +27 | |
|---|---|
| **Input** | **Output** |
| 1 | 28 |
| 11 | 38 |
| 16 | 43 |
| 23 | 53 |

**2.**

| Rule = −15 | |
|---|---|
| **Input** | **Output** |
| 25 | 10 |
| 19 | 4 |
| 15 | 0 |
| 13 | −2 |

**3.**

| Rule = +4 −3 | |
|---|---|
| **Input** | **Output** |
| 4 | 5 |
| 15 | 16 |
| 23 | 24 |
| 34 | 35 |

**4.**

| Rule = ×2 +3 | |
|---|---|
| **Input** | **Output** |
| 2 | 7 |
| 4 | 11 |
| 9 | 21 |
| 15 | 33 |

**5.**

| Rule = ÷2 +1 | |
|---|---|
| **Input** | **Output** |
| 4 | 3 |
| 16 | 9 |
| 24 | 13 |
| 38 | 20 |

**6.**

| Rule = ×3 −5 | |
|---|---|
| **Input** | **Output** |
| 19 | 52 |
| 15 | 40 |
| 8 | 19 |
| 1 | −2 |

**7.**

| Rule = ×3 −12 | |
|---|---|
| **Input** | **Output** |
| 12 | 24 |
| 8 | 12 |
| 5 | 3 |
| 3 | −3 |

**8.**

| Rule = ÷3 −2 | |
|---|---|
| **Input** | **Output** |
| 12 | 2 |
| 15 | 3 |
| 21 | 5 |
| 39 | 11 |

**9.**

| Rule = ×5 +1 | |
|---|---|
| **Input** | **Output** |
| 3 | 16 |
| 4 | 21 |
| 8 | 41 |
| 10 | 51 |

Deep Blue Sea

Simplify each of the following math expressions using the order of operations. Then write the corresponding letter on the line in front of the expression. The letters will spell out the solution to the riddle when read from bottom to top.

Skills:

Using Order of Operations to Solve Equations

## What is black and white and red all over?

### Order of Operations

1. Do whatever is inside the parentheses first.

2. Next, do multiplication and/or division from left to right.

3. The last step is to do addition and/or subtraction from left to right.

| | |
|---|---|
| 27 **A** | 14 **M** |
| 0 **B** | 5 **N** |
| 22 **C** | 17 **O** |
| 54 **D** | 19 **R** |
| 24 **E** | 15 **S** |

_____ $15 + 6 \times 2 =$ _____

_____ $20 + 10 \div 5 =$ _____

_____ $9 + 2 \times 5 =$ _____

_____ $14 + 1 \times 3 =$ _____

_____ $18 \times 6 \div 2 =$ _____

_____ $6 \times (3 + 1) =$ _____

_____ $16 - 4 \div 4 =$ _____

_____ $7 + 4 \times 2 =$ _____

_____ $33 - 3 \times 2 =$ _____

_____ $5 \times 2 + 9 =$ _____

_____ $26 - (9 - 2) =$ _____

_____ $8 \times 4 - 5 =$ _____

_____ $15 \times (3 - 3) =$ _____

_____ $19 - (10 - 5) =$ _____

_____ $26 - 6 \div 3 =$ _____

_____ $12 \div 3 + 1 =$ _____

_____ $30 - 9 \div 3 =$ _____

**Deep Blue Sea**

# What's the Order?

**1.** Timothy solved the following two problems and says that they have the same answer.

**a)** $5 \times 4 - 3 + 2 =$  

$20 - 5 = 15$

**b)** $5 \times 4 - (3 + 2) =$  

$20 - 5 = 15$

Do you agree with Timothy? Write him a note stating if you agree or not and why. Include in your note the correct answer for each problem.

_____

_____

**2.** Francine saw the following problem and was confused about the parentheses.

$7 + (5 \times 3) - 8$

She understood the order of operations, but was asked the question, "Are the parentheses necessary in this problem? If the parentheses were gone, wouldn't you solve the problem the same way?" Please write a note to Francine stating if you agree or not with her thinking and why. Include in your note the correct answer for the problem.

_____

_____

**3.** Drew saw the following problem and was confused about where to start.

$90 - (5 + 4 \times 3) + 30$

He knew that he should start inside the parentheses, but didn't know what he should do first, $5 + 4$ or $4 \times 3$. Write a note to Drew stating the steps he should follow to solve the problem. Include in your note the correct solution and answer for the problem.

_____

_____

Deep Blue Sea

Use the number line to help order the following ten numbers from smallest to largest. First, place each point on the number line and label it. After all the points have been plotted on the number line, list the numbers in order from smallest to largest.

$3\frac{1}{4}$   $4\frac{3}{4}$   $6\frac{3}{4}$

$6\frac{1}{3}$   $5\frac{1}{3}$   $5\frac{1}{4}$

$3\frac{1}{2}$   $6\frac{2}{3}$   $4\frac{2}{3}$

$5\frac{1}{2}$

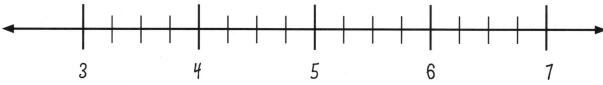

3   4   5   6   7

Deep Blue Sea

# Whale-Watching Trip

**Skills:**

Multiplying
and Dividing
Decimal
Numbers

Completing a
Chart

Each group agreed to share the cost of different whale-watching trips equally. How much did each person pay?

Fill in the missing numbers.

| Total Cost | Number of People in the Group | Each Person in the Group Paid |
|---|---|---|
| $18.75 | five | $_____ |
| $43.50 | three | $_____ |
| $31.40 | four | $_____ |
| $_____ | twenty | $7.32 |
| $_____ | eight | $6.55 |
| $93.50 | eleven | $_____ |
| $_____ | fifteen | $90.00 |
| $_____ | six | $14.25 |
| $144.00 | twelve | $_____ |

# How Deep Is the Ocean?

The chart below contains the deepest depths of four of the Earth's oceans. The numbers have been rounded to the nearest thousand. Use the information to complete the bar graph.

**Skills:**

Interpreting a Chart

Constructing a Bar Graph

| Pacific Ocean | Mariana Trench | 36,000 feet deep |
|---|---|---|
| Arctic Ocean | Eurasia Basin | 18,000 feet deep |
| Atlantic Ocean | Puerto Rico Trench | 28,000 feet deep |
| Indian Ocean | Java Trench | 25,000 feet deep |

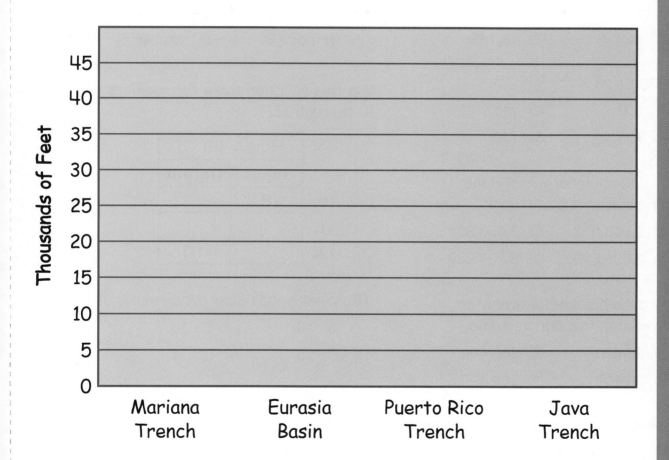

How much deeper is the deepest part of the Pacific Ocean than the deepest part of the Indian Ocean?

**TEST YOUR SKILLS**

Fill in the circle next to the correct answer.

**1.** 4,268 + 8,230 = _____
- Ⓐ 12,984
- Ⓒ 12,498
- Ⓑ 12,849
- Ⓓ 12,598

**2.** 2,631 − 1,320 = _____
- Ⓐ 1,321
- Ⓒ 1,311
- Ⓑ 1,211
- Ⓓ 1,221

**3.** 425 × 31 = _____
- Ⓐ 13,175
- Ⓒ 13,075
- Ⓑ 14,175
- Ⓓ 13,165

**4.** 2,750 ÷ 25 = _____
- Ⓐ 100
- Ⓒ 115
- Ⓑ 125
- Ⓓ 110

**5.** Find the number with 5 in the ten thousands place.
- Ⓐ 2,563,822
- Ⓒ 2,653,822
- Ⓑ 2,635,822
- Ⓓ 5,234,822

**6.** Find the number for twenty-six thousand, four hundred nine.
- Ⓐ 26,490
- Ⓒ 260,409
- Ⓑ 26,409
- Ⓓ 260,490

**7.** What is the expanded form of 3,287?
- Ⓐ 3,000 + 200 + 70 + 8
- Ⓑ 300 + 200 + 8 + 7
- Ⓒ 3,000 + 200 + 80 + 70
- Ⓓ 3,000 + 200 + 80 + 7

**8.** 7 × (5 + 2) = _____
- Ⓐ 7
- Ⓒ 49
- Ⓑ 37
- Ⓓ 56

**9.** Where does $4\frac{3}{4}$ belong on the number line?

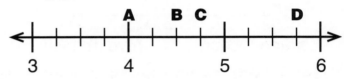

- Ⓐ point **A**
- Ⓒ point **C**
- Ⓑ point **B**
- Ⓓ point **D**

Use this function table for numbers 10 through 12.

| Rule = ×3 −5 | |
| --- | --- |
| **Input** | **Output** |
| **10.** 6 | |
| **11.** 1 | |
| **12.** | 10 |

**10.** What is the output if the input is 6?
- Ⓐ 18
- Ⓒ 13
- Ⓑ 23
- Ⓓ 4

**11.** What is the output if the input is 1?
- Ⓐ 3
- Ⓒ 8
- Ⓑ 2
- Ⓓ −2

**12.** What is the input if the output is 10?
- Ⓐ 5
- Ⓒ 15
- Ⓑ 10
- Ⓓ 20

**Skills:**

Reading a
Double-Bar
Graph

Demonstrating
Computation
Skills

The following graph shows the favorite collections of students in the sixth grade at Lincoln School.

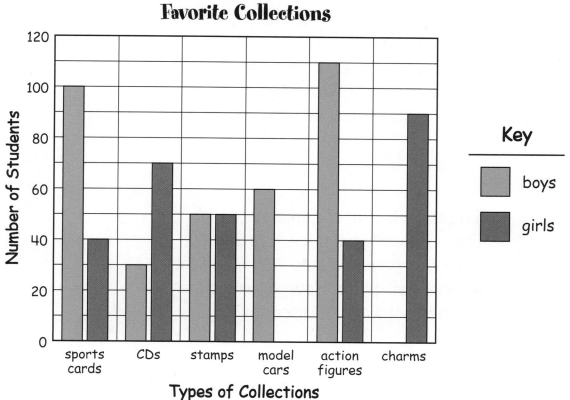

**Favorite Collections**

1. If each student could name only one type of collection, what is the total number of students shown on this graph?

   _____

2. Are more boys or girls represented on the graph? How many more?

   _____

3. Is it accurate to say that twice as many boys collect sports cards as collect model cars? Explain your answer.

   _____

4. Is it accurate to say that half as many girls collect stamps as collect charms? Explain your answer.

   _____

Collections

# Baseball Cards

Skills:

Demonstrating
Computation
of Mixed
Numbers

Determining
Fractional Part
of a Whole
Number

Using Linear
Measurement

Solve each problem.

1. Karl's dad collected baseball cards when his children were very young. Now that his children are older, he wants to give each of his three children the same number of cards to start their own collections. He has 3,732 cards. How many cards should each child receive?

_____

2. Sam purchased a box of baseball cards for his collection. The original price was $22.80, but the store was having a sale with $\frac{1}{4}$ off the price of all baseball cards. How much did the baseball cards cost with the discount?

_____

3. Amy has $\frac{2}{5}$ as many baseball cards as her brother, Max. If Max has 250 cards, how many cards does Amy have?

_____

4. Ramon has 432 baseball cards. He decided to lay the cards end to end down the hallway to see how far they would stretch. Each card is $3\frac{1}{2}$ inches long. How many feet long is the line of cards?

_____

The following line graph represents the value of Jonathon's baseball card collection.

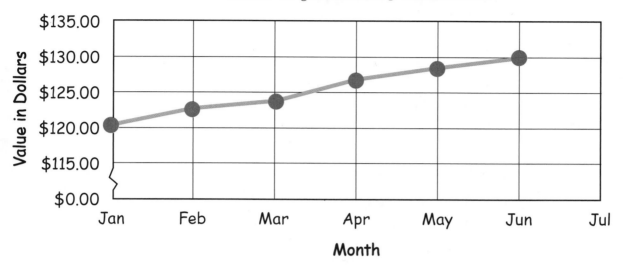

**Value of Jonathon's Collection**

Solve the problems.

1. How much has the value of Jonathon's collection increased from January to June?

   _____

2. If this trend continues, what would be a reasonable estimate for the value of his collection in July?

   _____

Collections

# Gabriela's Collection

**Skills:**

Demonstrating
Computation

Describing
Geometric
Shapes

Calculating
Elapsed Time

Solve the problems.

1. Gabriela has been saving her allowance to buy three CDs. Each CD costs $14.98. What will be the total for the CDs?

   _____

2. Gabriela is listening to her new CD. The time for each song is listed below.

   Song 1 — 4 minutes 22 seconds
   Song 2 — 5 minutes 11 seconds
   Song 3 — 3 minutes 26 seconds
   Song 4 — 9 minutes 58 seconds
   Song 5 — 7 minutes 3 seconds

   If she starts listening to the CD at 3:45 in the afternoon, at what time will the CD end?

   _____

3. Gabriela and Burt are looking at the shape of a CD. Gabriela says that CDs are shaped like a cone. Burt says that CDs are shaped like a cylinder. Which geometric term describes the shape of a CD? Explain why.

   _____

4. Gabriela prefers to buy CDs in sets of six. If she has 138 CDs from these sets, how many sets does she have?

   _____

5. Gabriela wants to give $\frac{1}{4}$ of her CDs to her younger sister. She has 240 CDs. How many will she give her sister?

   _____

The following graph represents the portion of the CD that each song uses.

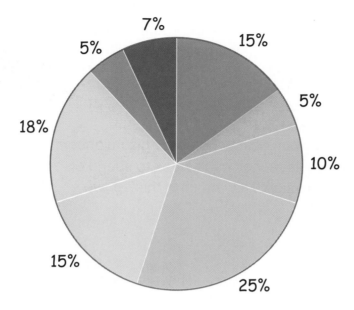

Solve each problem.

**1.** If the entire CD is one hour long, how many minutes long is 10 percent of the CD?

_____

**2.** If the entire CD is one hour long, how many minutes long is 18 percent of the CD?

_____

**3.** If the entire CD is one hour long, how much longer is the longest song than the shortest song?

_____

Collections

# Martin's Collection

Martin collects model cars. Solve these problems about his collection.

**1.** Martin has three dozen model cars. One-third of his collection used to belong to his older brother, Ralph. How many model cars did Ralph give to Martin?

_____

**2.** Martin earns $15 a week doing chores for his neighbors. Martin saves $\frac{1}{4}$ of this money each week to spend on new cars for his collection. How much is this?

_____

**3.** If Martin saved the same amount each week for one year (52 weeks), how much money would he have?

_____

**4.** This line graph shows how many model cars Martin had at the end of six months. Read the graph, and then answer the questions.

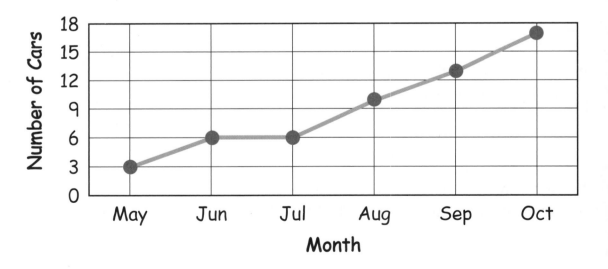

In which month did Martin buy no cars? _____

If the average cost of a model car was $2.50, how much did Martin spend?

_____

collections

Plot the ordered pairs of numbers in the order in which they are listed and connect them with straight lines. Start each new set of points with a new line. The first line has been drawn.

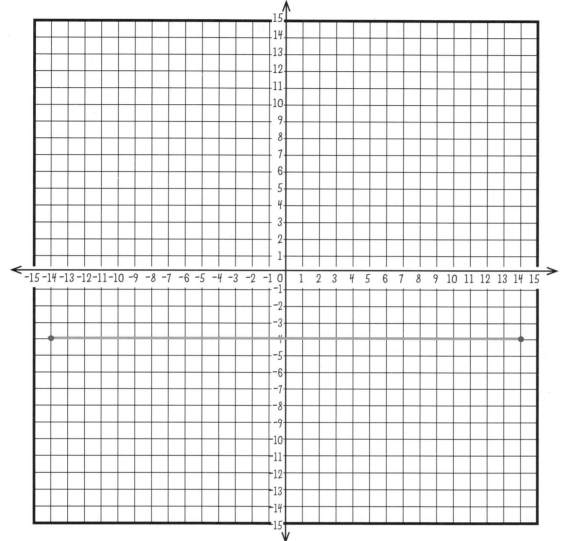

▸ (−14, −4) (14, −4) line ends

▸ (−9, −2) (−8, −4) (−6, −4) (−5, −2) line ends

▸ (−8, −2) (−7, −3) (−6, −2) line ends

▸ (5, −2) (6, −4) (8, −4) (9, −2) line ends

▸ (6, −2) (7, −3) (8, −2) line ends

▸ (2, 4) (2, −2) line ends

▸ (8, 1) (5, 3) (3, 3) (3, 1) (8, 1) line ends

▸ (1, 1) (1, 3) (−2, 3) (−4, 1) (1, 1) line ends

▸ (11, −1) (13, −1) (13, −2) (−11, −2) (−11, 0) (−10, 1) (−6, 1) (−2, 4) (5, 4) (9, 1) (11, 1) (11, −2) line ends

**Collections**

# Stamp Collections

Skills:

Solving One-
and Two-Step
Problems

Calculating
with
Percentages

Solve these problems.

1. Rick and Myra collect stamps. Rick has
   150 fewer stamps than Myra. Together they
   have collected 500 stamps. How many stamps
   does each person have in his or her collection?

   _____

2. Myra bought a new sheet of stamps that had
   10 thirty-seven cent stamps on the page. If she
   paid with a ten-dollar bill, how much change did
   she get back?

   _____

3. Rick has a stamp in his collection that his
   grandfather purchased for 24¢. The value of
   the stamp is now 300% of the original value.
   What is the current value of the stamp?

   _____

4. Myra has 150 stamps from foreign lands. $\frac{3}{5}$ of
   the stamps are from countries in Europe. How
   many European stamps does she have?

   _____

# Storage Boxes

The children keep their collections in storage boxes of different sizes. Calculate the volume of each box.

**Skills:**

Calculating Volume

### Do You Remember?

**Volume** is the amount of space in a 3-D shape.

volume of a rectangular prism or a cube =
length × width × height

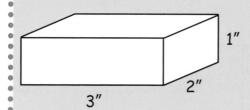

3″ × 2″ × 1″ = 6 cubic inches

**1.** Myra's storage box

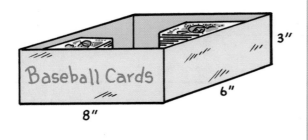

_____ × _____ × _____ =

_____ cubic inches

**2.** Gabriela's storage box

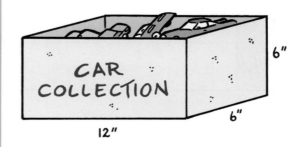

_____ × _____ × _____ =

_____ cubic inches

**3.** Karl's storage box

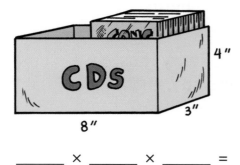

_____ × _____ × _____ =

_____ cubic inches

**4.** Martin's storage box

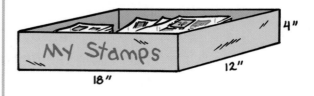

_____ × _____ × _____ =

_____ cubic inches

Collections

©2005 by Evan-Moor Corp. • EMC 4550 • Math

**UNIT 2**

**23**

# Stamp Collections

Erik, Jerry, Carol, and Sandy all collect stamps. They have their stamp collections stored in books that are different colors. Use the clues below to determine the color of each person's book and the number of stamps each book contains.

When you know that a person and a color or a person and a number of stamps do <u>not</u> go with each other, make an X under the color or number of stamps and across from that person's name. When you know that a person and color or a person and number of stamps do go together, write YES in that box.

|  | Black | Blue | Green | Red | 315 | 720 | 1,205 | 2,403 |
|---|---|---|---|---|---|---|---|---|
| Erik |  |  |  |  |  |  |  |  |
| Jerry |  |  |  |  |  |  |  |  |
| Carol |  |  |  |  |  |  |  |  |
| Sandy |  |  |  |  |  |  |  |  |

## Clues:

1. Carol has 1,205 stamps.
2. Sandy has the black book.
3. Neither Erik nor Jerry has the green book.
4. Erik has the red book.
5. The blue book contains the most stamps.
6. One of the boys (Erik or Jerry) has the fewest number of stamps, and the other has the largest number of stamps.
7. Jerry has more stamps than Erik.

# Percents

**Skills:**

Calculating
Percent of a
Whole Number

Find the percent of each stamp collection that is new.

**1.** What is 100% of 25?  _____

**2.** What is 10% of 60?  _____

**3.** What is 25% of 48?  _____

**4.** What is 70% of 50?  _____

**5.** What is 75% of 32?  _____

**6.** What is 90% of 40?  _____

**7.** What is 20% of 35?  _____

**8.** What is 50% of 32?  _____

**9.** What is 100% of 42?  _____

**10.** What is 25% of 20?  _____

**11.** What is 70% of 90?  _____

**12.** What is 75% of 36?  _____

**13.** What is 10% of 50?  _____

**14.** What is 10% of 70?  _____

**15.** What is 40% of 60?  _____

**16.** What is 90% of 70?  _____

> **Remember:**
>
> To find a percent of a number, multiply the number by the percent written in its decimal form.
>
> For example:
>
> 25% of 8
> $0.25 \times 8 = 2$
>
> 10% of 35
> $0.10 \times 35 = 3.5$

**Collections**

©2005 by Evan-Moor Corp. • EMC 4550 • Math

UNIT 2       **25**

# On Sale!

**Skills:**

Calculating Percent of Whole Numbers and Decimals

Solve each problem. Be sure to show your work on each problem.

**1.** Jonathon found a new scrapbook for his stamp collection. The original price was $36. The tag said it was 25% off. What was the sale price?

________________________

**2.** Gabriela was shopping at a store that advertised 50% off everything. She found a new CD player originally priced at $76. What was the sale price?

________________________

**3.** Every set of baseball cards was on sale at 20% off. The original price was $2.50. Karl bought three sets of cards. How much did he spend?

________________________

**4.** Martin found a case for his model car collection that was 30% off the original price of $60. How much did Martin save?

________________________

Fill in the circle next to the correct answer.

**1.** Seth bought baseball cards in sets of 6 for his collection. If he has 384 cards, how many sets has he bought?

Ⓐ 46    Ⓒ 48
Ⓑ 64    Ⓓ 84

**2.** Sam has $\frac{3}{5}$ as many baseball cards as Alex. If Alex has 250 cards, how many cards does Sam have?

Ⓐ 50    Ⓒ 100
Ⓑ 200    Ⓓ 150

**3.** What is 100% of 25?

Ⓐ 25    Ⓒ 20
Ⓑ 5    Ⓓ 50

**4.** What is 25% of 24?

Ⓐ 25    Ⓒ 6
Ⓑ 12    Ⓓ 4

**5.** What is 80% of 40?

Ⓐ 32    Ⓒ 30
Ⓑ 40    Ⓓ 20

**6.** What is 10% of 100?

Ⓐ 10    Ⓒ 50
Ⓑ 20    Ⓓ 90

Use the following four figures to answer numbers 7 and 8.

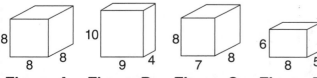

Figure A    Figure B    Figure C    Figure D

**7.** Which figure has a volume of 240 cubic inches?

Ⓐ Figure A    Ⓒ Figure C
Ⓑ Figure B    Ⓓ Figure D

**8.** Which figure has a volume of 360 cubic inches?

Ⓐ Figure A    Ⓒ Figure C
Ⓑ Figure B    Ⓓ Figure D

Use the following line graph to answer numbers 9 through 12.

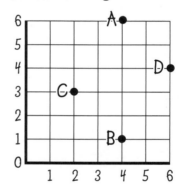

**9.** Which point is located at (4, 6)?

Ⓐ point A    Ⓒ point C
Ⓑ point B    Ⓓ point D

**10.** Which point is located at (2, 3)?

Ⓐ point A    Ⓒ point C
Ⓑ point B    Ⓓ point D

**11.** Which point is located at (6, 4)?

Ⓐ point A    Ⓒ point C
Ⓑ point B    Ⓓ point D

**12.** Plot point W at (3, 5) and point Z at (4, 3) on this graph.

# Win a Pizza!

**Skills:**

Multiplication of Fractions Including Mixed Numbers

The local pizza parlor is giving away a pizza to anyone who can answer all of these multiplication problems. Marcos wants to win. Can you give him a helping hand to find the correct answers? Write the answers in the simplest form.

1. $\frac{2}{5} \times \frac{1}{3} =$ _____

2. $\frac{1}{4} \times \frac{3}{7} =$ _____

3. $\frac{1}{2} \times \frac{3}{8} =$ _____

4. $\frac{3}{7} \times \frac{3}{4} =$ _____

5. $\frac{5}{9} \times \frac{1}{3} =$ _____

6. $1\frac{2}{5} \times 3\frac{3}{4} =$ _____

7. $4\frac{2}{7} \times \frac{1}{2} =$ _____

8. $3\frac{3}{5} \times 2\frac{6}{7} =$ _____

9. $1\frac{2}{5} \times 2\frac{3}{4} =$ _____

10. $4\frac{1}{2} \times 3\frac{1}{2} =$ _____

### Remember:

To multiply fractions, multiply the numerators, then multiply the denominators.

$$\frac{1}{2} \times \frac{2}{3} = \mathbf{?}$$

$$\frac{1 \times 2}{2 \times 3} = \frac{2}{6}$$

Reduce $\frac{2}{6}$ to simplest terms.

$$\frac{2}{6} = \mathbf{?}$$

$$\frac{2 \div 2}{6 \div 2} = \frac{1}{3}$$

To multiply mixed numbers by fractions, change the mixed numbers to improper fractions.

$$2\frac{1}{2} \times 2\frac{2}{3} = \mathbf{?}$$

$$\frac{5}{2} \times \frac{8}{3} =$$

Then multiply the fractions.

$$\frac{5 \times 8}{2 \times 3} = \frac{40}{6}$$

$$\frac{40}{6} = 6\frac{4}{6} = 6\frac{2}{3}$$

Math • EMC 4550 • ©2005 by Evan-Moor Corp.

# Tongue Twister

Complete each division problem below. Then write the corresponding letter on the line in front of each problem. The letters will spell out a tongue twister. Try to say it quickly six times.

*S*    $\frac{3}{4} \div \frac{1}{2} =$   $1\frac{1}{2}$

_____    $\frac{1}{2} \div \frac{2}{3} =$ _____

_____    $\frac{4}{5} \div \frac{3}{5} =$ _____

_____    $\frac{2}{3} \div \frac{5}{6} =$ _____

_____    $\frac{4}{7} \div \frac{1}{2} =$ _____

_____    $\frac{2}{4} \div \frac{2}{3} =$ _____

_____    $\frac{8}{10} \div \frac{3}{5} =$ _____

_____    $\frac{3}{4} \div \frac{1}{3} =$ _____

_____    $\frac{6}{8} \div \frac{1}{3} =$ _____

_____    $\frac{4}{5} \div \frac{2}{5} =$ _____

| | |
|---|---|
| $1\frac{1}{2}$ | **S** |
| $2$ | **A** |
| $\frac{4}{5}$ | **C** |
| $1\frac{1}{7}$ | **Y** |
| $1\frac{1}{3}$ | **I** |
| $2\frac{1}{4}$ | **Z** |
| $\frac{3}{4}$ | **P** |

### Remember:

To divide fractions, invert (turn upside down) the divisor fraction. Then multiply the fractions. Write the answer in the lowest terms.

**For example,**

$\frac{2}{3} \div \frac{1}{3} = ?$          $\frac{5}{6} \div \frac{2}{3} = ?$

$\frac{2}{3} \times \frac{3}{1} = \frac{6}{3}$         $\frac{5}{6} \times \frac{3}{2} = \frac{15}{12}$

$\frac{6}{3} = 2$            $\frac{15}{12} = 1\frac{3}{12} = 1\frac{1}{4}$

**Pizza Party**

# Pizza Parlor

**Solve each problem.**

1. Tim has one-half of a pizza that he wants to divide equally between two people. Draw a picture of this problem and tell how much pizza each person will get. Write the math sentence that goes with the problem.

   _____

2. George has three-fourths of a pizza. He is going to divide it into six equal pieces. Draw a picture of this problem and tell how much of the whole pizza each slice will be. Write the math sentence that goes with the problem.

   _____

3. Kelley has two whole pizzas. She is going to divide each pizza into pieces that are one-third of a whole pizza. Draw a picture of this problem and tell how many pieces she can make. Write the math sentence that goes with the problem.

   _____

4. Linda has five and one-third pizzas. She is going to divide them between some people who each request one and one-third pizzas. Draw a picture of this problem and tell how many one and one-third pizzas she can make. Write the math sentence that goes with the problem.

   _____

## Remember:

To divide a fraction by a whole number, change the whole number to an improper fraction with a denominator of one. Invert the divisor fraction and multiply.

$$\frac{1}{3} \div 3 = \, ?$$

$$\frac{1}{3} \div \frac{3}{1} =$$

$$\frac{1}{3} \times \frac{1}{3} = \frac{1}{9}$$

To divide a whole number by a fraction, change the whole number to an improper fraction with a denominator of one. Invert the divisor fraction and multiply.

$$6 \div \frac{3}{4} = \, ?$$

$$\frac{6}{1} \div \frac{3}{4} =$$

$$\frac{6}{1} \times \frac{4}{3} = \frac{24}{3} = 8$$

**Pizza Party**

Jake invited 11 of his friends to his birthday party at Antonio's Pizza Parlor. Use the information on the chart to help you solve the problems.

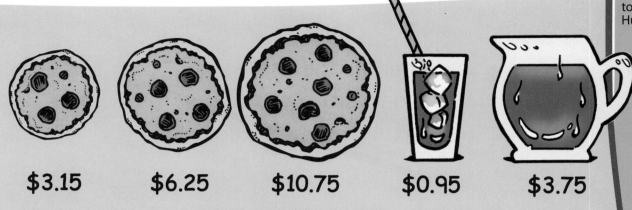

| $3.15 | $6.25 | $10.75 | $0.95 | $3.75 |

1. Jake ordered the following. How much did it cost?

   • 4 large pepperoni pizzas
   • 3 pitchers of cola

   _____

2. Each pizza was cut into 12 pieces. Each child ate $\frac{1}{4}$ of a pizza. How many pieces did each child eat?

   _____

3. Jake decided to take a medium cheese pizza and a small vegetable pizza home to his family. How much did this cost?

   _____

4. What is the difference between what Jake spent for the party and the cost of the pizzas he bought to take home?

   _____

**Skills:**

Multiplication of Decimals to the Hundredths

To figure out the answer, solve each of the multiplication problems below. Write the letter that corresponds to the answer on the line in front of each problem. The letters will spell out the answer.

Where is the best place to eat a pizza?

**Pizza Party**

__I__  $0.7 \times 0.4 =$ __0.28__

_____  $0.2 \times 0.3 =$ _____

_____  $0.9 \times 0.4 =$ _____

_____  $1.2 \times 0.6 =$ _____

_____  $4.3 \times 0.09 =$ _____

_____  $1.2 \times 1.3 =$ _____

_____  $5.1 \times 2.6 =$ _____

_____  $0.36 \times 2 =$ _____

_____  $1.29 \times 0.3 =$ _____

_____  $1.8 \times 6.4 =$ _____

_____  $0.17 \times 2.1 =$ _____

| | |
|---|---|
| 0.357 | **H** |
| 0.28 | **I** |
| 13.26 | **M** |
| 0.06 | **N** |
| 0.72 | **O** |
| 1.56 | **R** |
| 11.52 | **T** |
| 0.387 | **U** |
| 0.36 | **Y** |

# Decimal Division

Complete each of the following division problems. Do not give a remainder! Continue dividing until you get a decimal answer.

**1.** $2.1\overline{)6.72}$

**2.** $5.0\overline{)23}$

**3.** $3.43\overline{)17.836}$

**4.** $0.24\overline{)1.5696}$

**5.** $6.16\overline{)13.552}$

**6.** $4.99\overline{)1.1477}$

**7.** $98.0\overline{)10.78}$

**8.** $0.96\overline{)192}$

---

**Remember:**

When both the number you are dividing by (divisor) and the number you are dividing into (dividend) contain decimals, follow these steps.

**1.** Count the number of decimal places in the divisor.

$$\overset{1}{\overbrace{\phantom{2}}}$$
$$2.1\overline{)6.72}$$

**2.** Move the decimal point that many places right in the divisor and in the dividend.

$$2.1\overline{)6.72} = 21\overline{)67.2}$$

**3.** Place a decimal point in the answer (quotient) above the decimal point in the dividend.

$$21\overline{)67.2}$$

Pizza Party

# Finding Factors

**Skills:**

Calculating Prime Factorization for Numbers

You can find the prime factorization of a number by dividing by prime numbers as shown below.

```
2 | 12
  |----
2 |  6
  |----
     3
```

The prime factorization of 12 is 2 x 2 x 3.

| | | |
|---|---|---|
| **1.** 18 | **2.** 20 | **3.** 24 |
| **4.** 15 | **5.** 30 | **6.** 22 |

**Remember:**

**Prime numbers** are counting numbers that can be divided by only two numbers—1 and themselves. They can also be called counting numbers with only two factors.

These are the prime numbers to 53:

2 3 5 7 11 13 17 19 23 29 31 37 41 47 53

Pizza Party

Find the Greatest Common Factor (GCF) for each of the following sets of numbers.

**1.** 2, 4 = _____

**2.** 3, 9 = _____

**3.** 5, 15 = _____

**4.** 4, 12 = _____

**5.** 6, 8 = _____

**6.** 5, 10, 25 = _____

**7.** 6, 10, 18 = _____

**8.** 12, 24, 48 = _____

## Remember:

**Factors** are numbers that when multiplied together make a new number.

   3 and 4 are factors that when multiplied make 12.

**Common factors** are numbers that are factors of two or more numbers.

   3 is a common factor of both 6 and 12.

   4 is a common factor of both 8 and 14.

The **Greatest Common Factor (GCF)** is the largest common factor of two or more numbers.

   2, 3, 4, 6, and 12 are all common factors of 12 and 24.

   12 is the GCF of the two numbers.

   4, 8, 16 are common factors of 16 and 32.

   16 is the GCF of the two numbers.

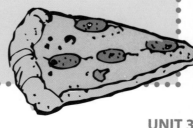

**Pizza Party**

# Reducing Fractions

**Skills:**

Calculating
the Greatest
Common
Factor

Reducing
Fractions to
Their Lowest
Terms

One way to reduce fractions to their lowest terms is to find the GCF of the numerator and the denominator. Then divide both by the GCF and you have reduced the fraction into its lowest terms.

> The GCF of 4 and 20 is 4. Divide both the numerator and denominator by 4.
>
> $$\frac{4}{20} = \frac{4 \div 4}{20 \div 4} = \frac{1}{5}$$

Find the GCF of each numerator and denominator and reduce the fraction.

1. $\frac{3}{9}$ = _____

2. $\frac{4}{12}$ = _____

3. $\frac{5}{10}$ = _____

4. $\frac{15}{20}$ = _____

5. $\frac{4}{7}$ = _____

6. $\frac{2}{6}$ = _____

7. $\frac{12}{15}$ = _____

8. $\frac{20}{24}$ = _____

9. $\frac{15}{45}$ = _____

10. $\frac{36}{42}$ = _____

Pizza Party

# Ordering Decimals

Use the number line to help order the following 10 numbers from smallest to largest. First, place each point on the number line and label it. After all the points have been plotted on the number line, list the numbers in order from smallest to largest.

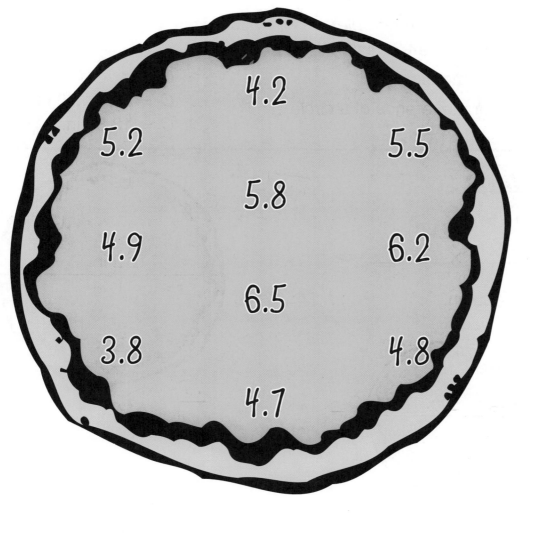

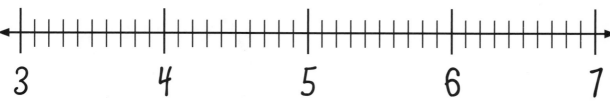

**Pizza Party**

# How Big Is It?

Use the formula below to find the circumference (distance around the circle) of each pizza.

$$C = \pi \times d$$

$\pi$ = pi (pronounced *pie*)
   pi is about 3.14

$d$ = diameter

$C$ = circumference of a circle

6 in.

$C = \pi \times d$
$C = 3.14 \times 6$ in.
$C = 18.84$ in.

**1.**

3 in.

_____ × _____ =

_____ in.

**2.**

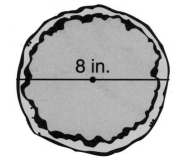

8 in.

_____ × _____ =

_____ in.

**3.**

4 in.

_____ × _____ =

_____ in.

**4.**

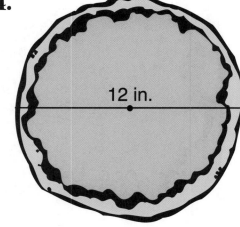

12 in.

_____ × _____ =

_____ in.

**5.**

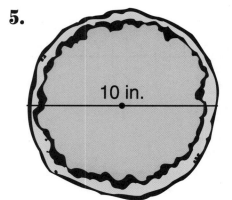

10 in.

_____ × _____ =

_____ in.

Pizza Party

Note: Use this assessment after your child has completed through page 38.

Fill in the circle next to the correct answer. If possible, simplify each fraction.

1. $\frac{1}{2} \times \frac{1}{3} =$ _____

   Ⓐ $\frac{1}{6}$  Ⓒ $\frac{2}{5}$

   Ⓑ $\frac{1}{2}$  Ⓓ $\frac{1}{3}$

2. $\frac{3}{5} \times \frac{2}{3} =$ _____

   Ⓐ $1\frac{1}{5}$  Ⓒ $1\frac{4}{15}$

   Ⓑ $\frac{2}{5}$  Ⓓ $2\frac{1}{2}$

3. $\frac{1}{2} \div \frac{1}{2} =$ _____

   Ⓐ $\frac{1}{2}$  Ⓒ 1

   Ⓑ 2  Ⓓ $\frac{2}{5}$

4. $\frac{2}{3} \div \frac{2}{5} =$ _____

   Ⓐ $\frac{4}{15}$  Ⓒ $1\frac{5}{6}$

   Ⓑ $1\frac{2}{3}$  Ⓓ $\frac{3}{5}$

5. $0.2 \times 3.0 =$ _____

   Ⓐ 6.0  Ⓒ 0.06

   Ⓑ 0.6  Ⓓ 0.23

6. $5.0 \times 0.4 =$ _____

   Ⓐ 0.2  Ⓒ 0.05

   Ⓑ 2.0  Ⓓ 0.02

7. $2.0\overline{)0.8}$

   Ⓐ 4.0  Ⓒ 40.0

   Ⓑ 0.04  Ⓓ 0.4

8. $0.3\overline{)9.0}$

   Ⓐ 3.0  Ⓒ 30.0

   Ⓑ 300.0  Ⓓ 0.3

9. What does GCF stand for?

   Ⓐ Greatest Continuous Figure

   Ⓑ Geometric Circular Figure

   Ⓒ General Combination Factor

   Ⓓ Greatest Common Factor

10. What is the GCF of 3 and 6?

   Ⓐ 1  Ⓒ 18

   Ⓑ 3  Ⓓ 6

11. What is the GCF of 8 and 12?

   Ⓐ 8  Ⓒ 4

   Ⓑ 2  Ⓓ 24

Use the following four figures to answer number 12.

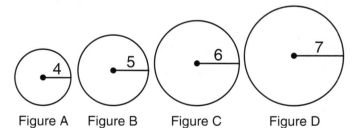

Figure A    Figure B    Figure C    Figure D

12. Which figure has a circumference of 31.4?

   Ⓐ Figure A  Ⓒ Figure C

   Ⓑ Figure B  Ⓓ Figure D

# Neighborhood Yard Sale

Solve these problems:

1. Ten families decided to have a neighborhood yard sale. They put an ad in the newspaper announcing that the sale would begin at 8:30 A.M. and end at 6:00 P.M. How long would the yard sale last?

   _____9:30_____

2. Alex picked out a kite for $1.75, a ball for $0.59, and a bat for $2.25. If he paid with a ten-dollar bill, how much change would he receive?

   $____5.41____

   1.75
   0.59
   +2.25
   _____
   4.59

   9 9
   10.00
   - 4.59
   _____
   5.41

3. What is the fewest number of bills and coins that Alex could receive as change? List them.

   $5 bill    one 25¢

   one dime    one Nickel    one 1¢

4. At the end of the day, the Lee family announced that all items were half price. If the sticker on a rocking chair read $21.50, how much would it sell for?

   ____10.75____

# Count the Money

The Galloway family recorded the amount of money that was collected at their garage sale.

| Person | Amount of Money Collected |
|---|---|
| Nancy | 45¢, $1, 75¢, $1.25 |
| John | $2, $2, $1.50, 25¢ |
| Susan | $5 |
| Scott | $3, $1.75, 30¢ |
| Judy | 90¢, 35¢, 75¢, 25¢, 10¢, 75¢ |

1. How much money did each family member make at the yard sale?

   Nancy _____        Scott _____

   John _____         Judy _____

   Susan _____

2. What was the average amount of money that the five people in the Galloway family collected during the garage sale?

   _____

> **Remember:**
>
> To find the **average**, add up the list of numbers and divide the sum by the number of items on the list.
>
> **For example,**
>
> 2, 5, 9, 12
>
> • The sum of the four numbers is 28.
> • 28 ÷ 4 = 7
> • The average of the four numbers is 7.

Yard Sale

# Lemonade Stand

Mark and Marta set up a lemonade stand at the neighborhood yard sale. They wanted to earn enough money to go to the movies with their friends. Their parents agreed to furnish the ice they would need, but the twins had to buy everything else.

1. The twins bought 12 cans of frozen lemonade that cost 99¢ a can. They also bought a package of 50 plastic cups that cost $2.99. How much money did they spend at the market?

   $11.88 + 14.8$

2. Each can of frozen lemonade makes 4 cups (1 quart) of lemonade. How many cups of lemonade will they be able to make with the 12 cans they bought?

   48 cups

3. Mark and Marta sold 36 glasses of lemonade at 50¢ a cup. Then they put the remaining lemonade on sale at $\frac{1}{2}$ price. They sold 9 cups at the sale price. How much money did they collect in all?

   20.25

4. How much profit did the twins make? 20.25

   $ 5.38

5. It costs $2.50 for a ticket to the movies. Did the twins make enough profit to pay for their movie tickets? Explain your answer.

   Yes, with 38¢ left ($0.38)

# Work Schedule

Complete the chart to show how long each person worked at the yard sale.

| | Person | Starting Time | Ending Time | Time Worked (in hours and minutes) |
|---|---|---|---|---|
| 1. | Alex | 7:07 A.M. | 10:45 A.M. | 3:38 |
| 2. | Mei Ling | 10:17 A.M. | 1:55 P.M. | 3:38 |
| 3. | Nancy | 8:13 A.M. | 12:41 P.M. | 4:28 |
| 4. | Ramon | 12:10 P.M. | 5:28 P.M. | 5:18 |
| 5. | Jamal | 9:03 A.M. | 12:03 P.M. | 3 hrs |
| 6. | Matt | 7:53 A.M. | 11:31 A.M. | 3:38 |
| 7. | Kay | 3:25 P.M. | 6:43 P.M. | 3:18 |
| 8. | Winston | 9:27 A.M. | 5:27 P.M. | 8:00 |

**9.** What is the difference between the longest time worked and the shortest time worked?

_____

Yard Sale

# Making Change

**Skills:**

Solve Multi-step Word Problems

Add, Subtract, and Multiply Amounts of Money

Calculate what each person spent and the amount of change each received back.

**1.** Receipt

$1.50

$0.25

$1.00

$0.50

**Total** _____

**Paid With** $5.00

**Change** _____

**2.** Receipt

3 items at
$2.00 each _____

4 items at
$1.00 each _____

2 items at
$0.50 each _____

**Total** _____

**Paid With** $20.00

**Change** _____

**3.** Receipt

$0.10

$0.50

$0.25

$1.00

$0.50

**Total** _____

**Paid With** $3.00

**Change** _____

**4.** Receipt

$2.00

$1.50

$1.00

$0.50

$0.25

**Total** _____

**Paid With** $10.00

**Change** _____

**5.** Receipt

$27.00

$4.50

$0.75

$1.00

$2.25

**Total** _____

**Paid With** $40.00

**Change** _____

**6.** Receipt

12 items at
$1.00 each _____

3 items at
$2.00 each _____

1 item at
$0.75 _____

2 items at
$0.50 each _____

**Total** _____

**Paid With** $20.00

**Change** _____

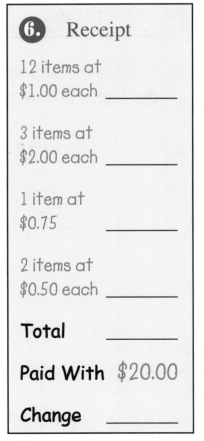

Yard Sale

# Miller's Front Yard

The Miller family wants to know how large their front yard is so they can decide how many tables to rent for the neighborhood yard sale. (Hint: You may need to divide the yard into two parts to find the area.)

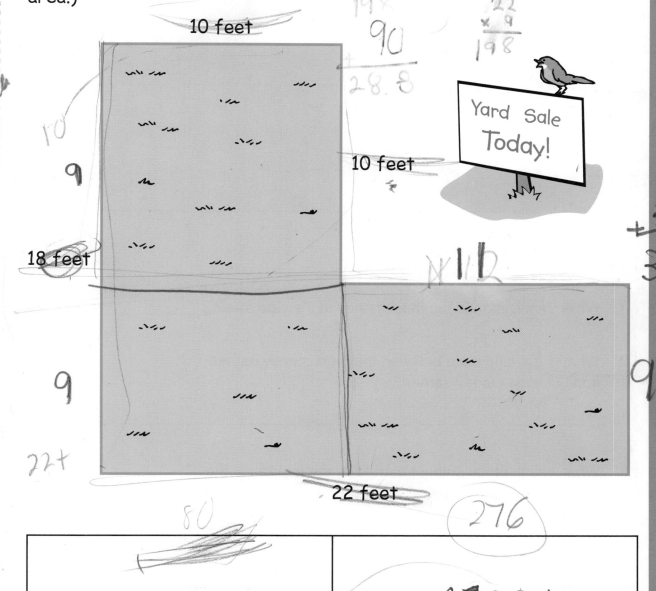

perimeter __80 feet__          area __276 feet__

```
Remember:

To find the perimeter of a rectangle, add the length of all sides.

To find the area of a shape, multiply the length by the width.
```

# A Successful Yard Sale

**Skills:**

Interpreting a Graph

Calculating Sums and Differences

Figuring an Average

Read the bar graph to answer the questions.

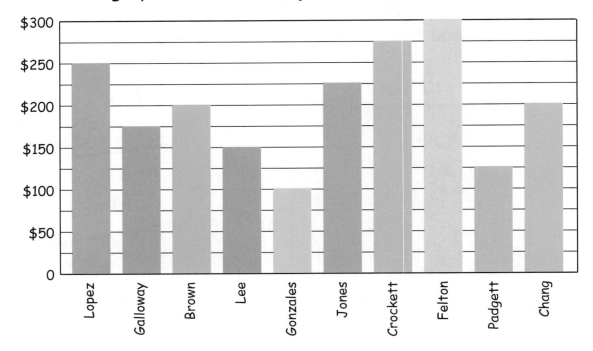

1. Which family earned the most money at the yard sale? _____

2. What is the difference between the most money earned and the least money earned?

   _____

3. What was the total amount earned by the families at the neighborhood yard sale?

   _____

4. What was the average amount earned by a family at the yard sale?

   _____

> **Remember:**
>
> To calculate an **average**, add all the items together and then divide by the number of items. For example 3, 5, 7, and 1.
>
> 16 is the sum of the numbers.
> 16 ÷ 4 = 4 is the average.

Yard Sale

Jacob made yard sale signs for some of his neighbors. Each sign was a different shape. Identify the shapes. Write the name of the correct shape under each sign. Write the family names on the correct signs.

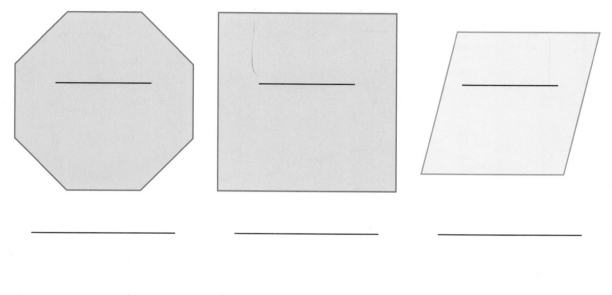

_____     _____     _____

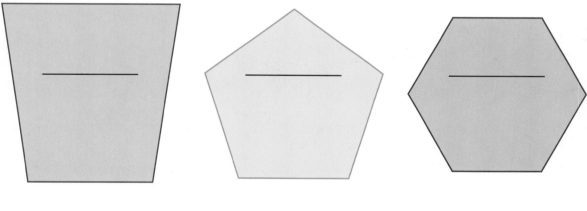

_____     _____     _____

The **Jones** family's sign is a **square**.

The **Gonzales** family's sign is a **rhombus**.

The **Lopez** family's sign is a **pentagon**.

The **Lee** family's sign is an **octagon**.

The **Brown** family's sign is a **trapezoid**.

The **Galloway** family's sign is a **hexagon**.

**Yard Sale**

# Pair Me Up

**Skills:**

Identifying
Congruent
Shapes

Arturo bought a book of math puzzles at the yard sale. Follow the directions to help Arturo complete this puzzle. Draw a line connecting the congruent shapes. The shapes might be flipped or turned. For each shape that doesn't have a partner, draw a congruent shape that is rotated 90 degrees.

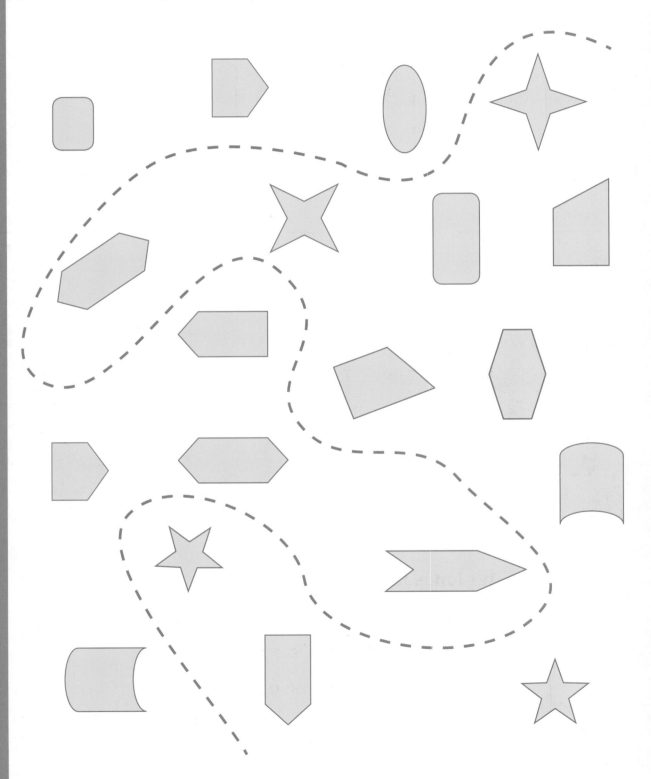

Yard Sale

# Transformations

**Skills:**

Identifying
Congruent
Shapes

Look at each pair of shapes. Determine how the shape is transformed from the one on the left to the one on the right.

1.   _____

2.   _____

3. 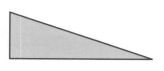  _____

4.   _____

5. 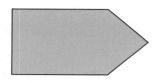 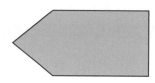 _____

6.   _____

7.   _____

8.  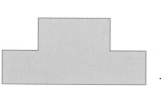 _____

**Yard Sale**

---

### Remember:

| Shapes can be changed in three ways: | **turned** (rotated) | **slid** (translated) | **flipped** (reflected) |
| --- | --- | --- | --- |
| |  |  |   |

©2005 by Evan-Moor Corp. • EMC 4550 • Math      **UNIT 4**

**49**

# What Did Carlos Buy?

Look at each figure in the box. Find the shape at the bottom of the page that is congruent (same shape and size) to the white region. Write the corresponding letter on the line above the congruent shape. The letters will spell out what Carlos bought at the neighborhood yard sale.

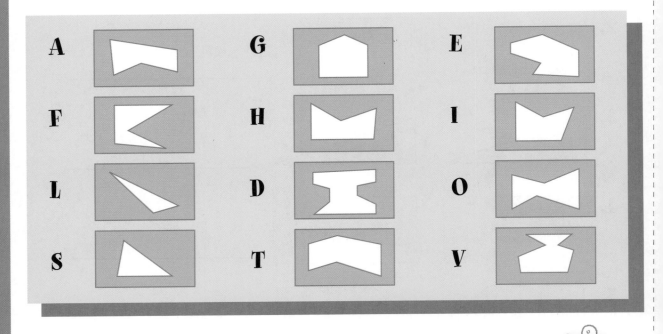

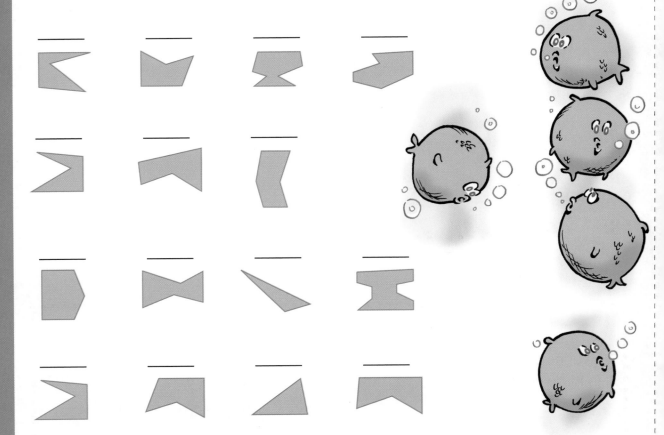

For each of the following figures, draw all the lines of symmetry. If there are line(s) of symmetry, write the number of lines next to the figure. If there are no lines of symmetry, write the word *none* next to the figure.

**1.** 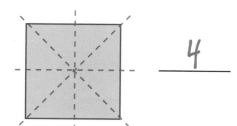  4

**5.** 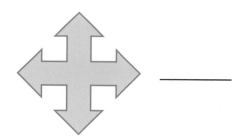  _____

**2.** 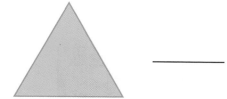  _____

**6.** 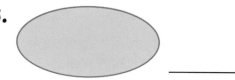  _____

**3.** 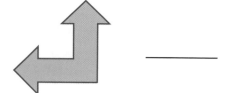  _____

**7.** 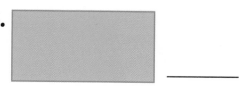  _____

**4.**   _____

**8.** 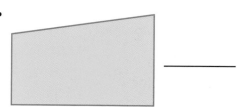  _____

### Remember:

If a shape could be folded on the line of symmetry, the two parts would match. Some shapes have many lines of symmetry. Some shapes have none.

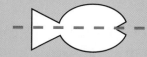

**1 line of symmetry**

**0 lines of symmetry**

©2005 by Evan-Moor Corp. • EMC 4550 • Math

Yard Sale

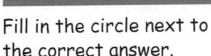

Fill in the circle next to the correct answer.

**1.** Deidre is buying 5 CDs for $14.95 each. What is the total cost of the CDs?

Ⓐ $75.75  Ⓒ $74.75
Ⓑ $74.05  Ⓓ $74.25

**2.** Pete paid $61.50 for six pizzas. How much did he pay for each pizza?

Ⓐ $11.50  Ⓒ $12.50
Ⓑ $6.75  Ⓓ $10.25

**3.** Irma bought three games. The prices were $4.50, $3.75, and $2.25. What was the average cost of a game?

Ⓐ $2.50  Ⓒ $3.75
Ⓑ $3.50  Ⓓ $4.25

**4.** How much time elapses between 4:45 A.M. and 6:17 A.M.?

Ⓐ 2 hours 32 minutes
Ⓑ 1 hour 28 minutes
Ⓒ 1 hour 32 minutes
Ⓓ 32 minutes

**5.** How much time elapses between 9:15 A.M. and 1:10 P.M.?

Ⓐ 1 hour 30 minutes
Ⓑ 13 hours 30 minutes
Ⓒ 3 hours and 55 minutes
Ⓓ 1 hour 15 minutes

**6.** Name the shape.

Ⓐ trapezoid
Ⓑ rhombus
Ⓒ rectangle
Ⓓ octagon

**For numbers 7 and 8, use these figures:**

A  B  C  D

**7.** Which figure is congruent to the white region?

Ⓐ figure A
Ⓑ figure B
Ⓒ figure C
Ⓓ figure D

**8.** Which figure is congruent to the white region?

Ⓐ figure A
Ⓑ figure B
Ⓒ figure C
Ⓓ figure D

**9.** How has this shape been transformed?

Ⓐ turned (rotated)
Ⓑ flipped (reflected)
Ⓒ slid (translated)
Ⓓ turned or slid

**10.** Write your name. Then slide your name to the right and write it again (label it *slide*).

**11.** What is the area of this figure?

Ⓐ 8.1 square units
Ⓑ 4.3 square units
Ⓒ 4.2 square units
Ⓓ 8.2 square units

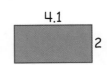

**12.** How many lines of symmetry does this figure have?

Ⓐ 1 line of symmetry
Ⓑ 2 lines of symmetry
Ⓒ 3 lines of symmetry
Ⓓ 4 lines of symmetry

To find the answer to this riddle, follow the steps below:

## What is bought by the yard and worn by the foot?

**1.** This table represents the sports students like to watch on TV. Use it to draw a double bar graph that represents the information on the empty graph below.

|  | Football | Basketball | Soccer | Baseball |
|---|---|---|---|---|
| **Boys** | 10 | 4 | 11 | 3 |
| **Girls** | 5 | 9 | 12 | 1 |

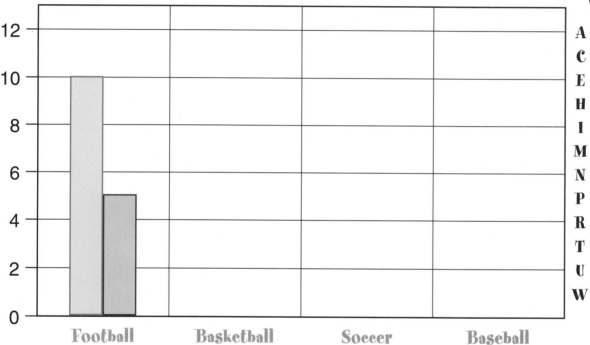

**2.** Each line below has a sport and a gender listed under it. This corresponds to one of the bars you drew on the graph. Go to the top of each bar and look horizontally to the right and you will see a letter. Write this letter on the corresponding line, and it will spell out the answer to the riddle.

| _____ | _____ | _____ | _____ | _____ | _____ |
|---|---|---|---|---|---|
| soccer boys | soccer girls | basketball boys | football girls | football boys | baseball boys |

# What's Your Range?

## Find the **range.**

**1.** 5, 7, 8, 8, 15, 23

_____

**2.** 42, 48, 53, 54, 57, 59, 60, 61, 61

_____

**3.** 22, 23, 26, 31, 38, 41, 45, 62

_____

### Remember:

*Range* is the difference between the greatest and the least number in a set of data.

21, 15, 27, 12, 20
27 − 12 = 15
The range is 15.

## Find the **mean.**

**7.** 5, 7, 8, 8, 15, 23

_____

**8.** 42, 48, 53, 54, 57, 59, 60, 61, 61

_____

**9.** 22, 23, 26, 31, 38, 41, 45, 62

_____

### Remember:

*Mean* is the average of a set of data. Add the numbers, then divide the sum of the numbers by the number of addends.

21 + 15 + 27 + 12 + 20 = 95
95 ÷ 5 = 19
The mean is 19.

## Find the **median.**

**4.** 5, 7, 8, 8, 15, 23

_____

**5.** 42, 48, 53, 54, 57, 59, 60, 61, 61

_____

**6.** 22, 23, 26, 31, 38, 41, 45, 62

_____

### Remember:

*Median* is the middle number in a set of data. Arrange the numbers from least to greatest. The middle number is the median.

12, 15, 20, 21, 27
The median is 20.

## Find the **mode.**

**10.** 5, 7, 8, 8, 15, 23

_____

**11.** 42, 48, 53, 54, 57, 59, 60, 61, 61

_____

**12.** 22, 23, 26, 31, 38, 41, 45, 62

_____

### Remember:

*Mode* is the number that appears the most often in a set of data. Some sets have no mode.

21, 15, 27, 12, 20
There is no mode.
23, 18, 6, 15, 6
The mode is 6.

**Play Ball**

Complete each of the following to make a true math sentence.

**Skills:**

Converting
Linear Units
of Customary
Measurement

**1.** 4 yards =  _____ feet

**2.** $25\frac{1}{3}$ yards = _____ feet

**3.** 24 inches = _____ feet

**4.** 17.5 feet = _____ inches

**5.** 21 feet = _____ yards

**6.** 33 feet = _____ yards

**7.** 5 yards = _____ inches

**8.** 50 yards = _____ feet

**9.** 81 feet = _____ yards

**10.** 288 inches = _____ yards

> **Remember:**
>
> 12 inches = 1 foot
>
> 3 feet = 1 yard

HOW FAR DID I HIT THE BALL?

**Play Ball**

# What's Happening?

Complete each math sentence below with a value that makes the sentence true. Then write the corresponding letter in front of the math sentences. The letters will spell out what has just happened in the football game.

**Remember:**

10 millimeters = 1 centimeter

100 centimeters = 1 meter

1,000 meters = 1 kilometer

| | |
|---|---|
| 40 | **A** |
| 100 | **C** |
| 1 | **D** |
| 3 | **H** |
| 4 | **N** |
| 2 | **O** |
| 10 | **T** |
| 50 | **U** |
| 6 | **W** |

_____  ☐ centimeters = 400 millimeters

_____  1,000 centimeters = ☐ meters

_____  ☐ meters = 200 centimeters

_____  ☐ meters = 5,000 centimeters

_____  ☐ centimeters = 1,000 millimeters

_____  30 millimeters = ☐ centimeters

_____  ☐ meter = 1,000 millimeters

_____  ☐ kilometers = 2,000 meters

_____  6,000 meters = ☐ kilometers

_____  ☐ kilometers = 4,000 meters

Math • EMC 4550 • ©2005 by Evan-Moor Corp.

**Skills:**
Calculating with Fractions (Addition, Subtraction, Multiplication, Division)

Complete each equation. Write the corresponding letter on the line above the answer. The letters will spell out the answer to the riddle.

Why did the police officer rush into the baseball game?

T  $\frac{2}{3} + \frac{3}{4} =$ _____

O  $\frac{1}{2} \times \frac{1}{2} =$ _____

S  $8\frac{1}{3} - 3\frac{1}{2} =$ _____

B  $\frac{2}{3} \div \frac{1}{3} =$ _____

M  $2\frac{1}{4} + 3\frac{1}{2} =$ _____

E  $\frac{6}{5} \div \frac{2}{3} =$ _____

A  $7\frac{1}{3} - 2 =$ _____

L  $2\frac{1}{2} \times 2\frac{2}{3} =$ _____

N  $9\frac{3}{4} - 4\frac{1}{2} =$ _____

D  $2\frac{2}{3} + 1\frac{2}{3} =$ _____

C  $\frac{1}{3} + \frac{1}{3} =$ _____

> **Remember:**
>
> To review rules for working with fractions, read these pages:
>
> page 28—multiplying fractions
>
> page 29—dividing fractions
>
> page 84—adding and subtracting fractions

\_\_\_\_\_  \_\_\_\_\_  \_\_\_\_\_  \_\_\_\_\_  \_\_\_\_\_  \_\_\_\_\_  \_\_\_\_\_
$4\frac{5}{6}$  $\frac{1}{4}$  $5\frac{3}{4}$  $1\frac{4}{5}$  $\frac{1}{4}$  $5\frac{1}{4}$  $1\frac{4}{5}$

\_\_\_\_\_  \_\_\_\_\_  \_\_\_\_\_  \_\_\_\_\_  \_\_\_\_\_
$4\frac{5}{6}$  $1\frac{5}{12}$  $\frac{1}{4}$  $6\frac{2}{3}$  $1\frac{4}{5}$

\_\_\_\_\_  \_\_\_\_\_  \_\_\_\_\_  \_\_\_\_\_  \_\_\_\_\_  \_\_\_\_\_
$4\frac{5}{6}$  $1\frac{4}{5}$  $\frac{2}{3}$  $\frac{1}{4}$  $5\frac{1}{4}$  $4\frac{1}{3}$

\_\_\_\_\_  \_\_\_\_\_  \_\_\_\_\_  \_\_\_\_\_
$2$  $5\frac{1}{3}$  $4\frac{5}{6}$  $1\frac{4}{5}$

**Play Ball**

# Basketball Jerseys

The basketball team wants new jerseys this year. They are trying to decide on which combination they would like. Here are their color choices:

- jersey color choices: red, blue, green, yellow, white
- name and letter color choices: black, purple, orange

Draw a tree diagram and tell how many combinations there are.

There are _____ combinations.

---

**Remember:**

A **tree diagram** is a way to show the number of different combinations that can be made from a set of information. Each "branch" lists one possible combination.

Here is an example using possible colors for cars and their interiors.

- two colors of paint (red and green)
- two colors of interiors (white and black)

Each branch lists one possible combination. There are a total of four different combinations on this tree diagram.

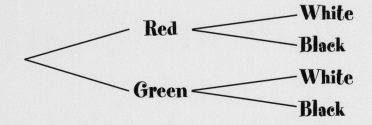

Play Ball

# Factor Trees

Factor trees can be used to find the prime factorization of any number. The following are examples of factor trees used to find the prime factorization of the number 18:

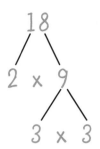
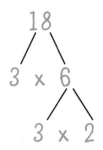

Draw a factor tree to find the prime factorization of each of the following numbers.

**1.** 15

**4.** 14

**7.** 25

**2.** 24

**5.** 45

**8.** 80

**3.** 32

**6.** 40

**9.** 16

# Football Field

**1.** Find the perimeter of the football field. _____

**2.** Find the area of the football field. _____

160 feet

360 feet

Play Ball

Use the order of operations as you solve these math expressions.

**10.** $9 \times 5 - (4 + 14) =$ _____

**9.** $9 \times 5 - 4 + 14 =$ _____

**8.** $15 \div (4 \times 6 \div 8) =$ _____

**7.** $8 + 4 \times 3 \div 2 =$ _____

**6.** $4 \times (5 + 6) \div 2 =$ _____

**5.** $4 \times 5 + 6 \div 2 =$ _____

**4.** $25 \div (10 - 5) =$ _____

**3.** $15 - (10 \div 2) =$ _____

**2.** $6 \div (6 - 3) =$ _____

**1.** $9 \times (5 \times 3) =$ _____

**Play Ball**

### Remember:

Follow these steps in using order of operations:

1. Do whatever is inside the parentheses first.

2. Next, do multiplication and/or division from left to right.

3. The last step is to do addition and/or subtraction from left to right.

# Make a Basket

Kim has scored in all eight of the basketball games she has played in so far this season. The chart shows how many points she made in each game. Record this information on the line graph below.

## Kim's Scoring Record

| | | | |
|---|---|---|---|
| Game 1 | 17 points | Game 5 | 11 points |
| Game 2 | 24 points | Game 6 | 24 points |
| Game 3 | 22 points | Game 7 | 30 points |
| Game 4 | 36 points | Game 8 | 27 points |

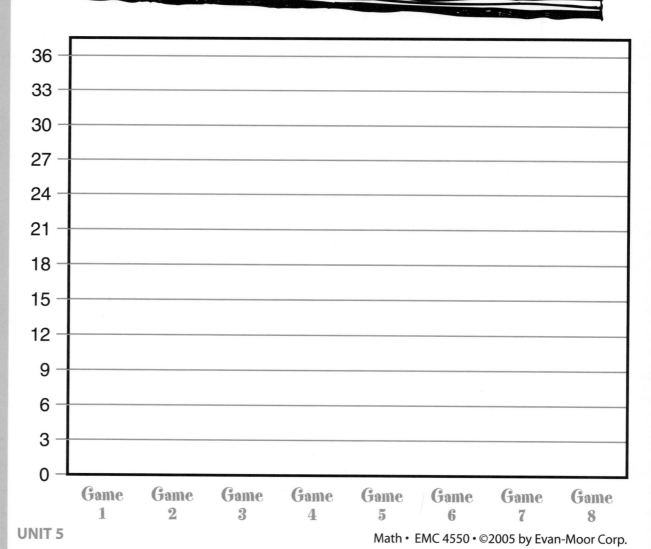

**Play Ball**

Math • EMC 4550 • ©2005 by Evan-Moor Corp.

Draw a straight line from each figure on the left to the correct number of faces that figure has. Each line will go through a number. Write the corresponding letter on the line above the number. The letters will answer the question.

**Skills:**

Identifying
Characteristics
of Three-
Dimensional
Solids

*What is the name of a favorite stadium treat?*

**O** =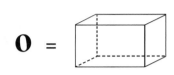

**S** =

**H** =

**G** =

**T** =

**D** =

**O** =

• 4 faces

• 5 faces

• 6 faces

• 7 faces

• 8 or more faces

1

5

7

6

4

3

2

___ ___ ___    ___ O ___ ___
1   2   3     4  5  6  7

Play Ball

**TEST YOUR SKILLS**

Fill in the circle next to the correct answer.

**1.** How many faces does this solid have?

Ⓐ 3

Ⓑ 4

Ⓒ 5

Ⓓ 6

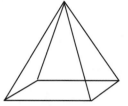

**2.** What is the perimeter of this figure?

Ⓐ 35 units

Ⓑ 42 units

Ⓒ 39 units

Ⓓ 46 units

10
7    3
8  2
5  3
8

**3.** What is the area of this figure?

Ⓐ 32 square units

Ⓑ 48 square units

Ⓒ 36 square units

Ⓓ 24 square units

4
8

**For numbers 4 through 7, use the following data:**

25, 30, 40, 50, 72, 83

**4.** What is the mean of the data?

Ⓐ 35        Ⓒ 50

Ⓑ 40        Ⓓ 45

**5.** What is the range of the data?

Ⓐ 58        Ⓒ 25

Ⓑ 62        Ⓓ 83

**6.** What is the mode of the data?

Ⓐ 25        Ⓒ 0

Ⓑ 30        Ⓓ There is no mode.

**7.** What is the median of the data?

Ⓐ 40        Ⓒ 45

Ⓑ 50        Ⓓ 83

**8.** Which of the following is equivalent to 12 feet?

Ⓐ 60 inches      Ⓒ 3 yards

Ⓑ 108 inches     Ⓓ 4 yards

**9.** Which of the following is equivalent to 10 millimeters?

Ⓐ 1 meter

Ⓑ 1 centimeter

Ⓒ 10 meters

Ⓓ 10 centimeters

**10.** $12 \div 3 + 4 \times 3 = $ _____

Ⓐ 4        Ⓒ 12

Ⓑ 16       Ⓓ 13

**11.** How many different single-scoop ice-cream cones can be made with two different kinds of ice-cream cones and three different flavors of ice cream?

Ⓐ 1        Ⓒ 3

Ⓑ 2        Ⓓ 6

**12.** Complete this factor tree.

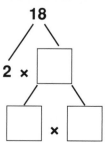

18

2 ×

×

# Points and Lines

Skills:

Identifying
Lines and Parts
of Lines

Identifying
Parallel and
Perpendicular
Lines

Name the following using words and then symbols.

**1.** X      Y
_____    _____
_____

**2.** Q      R
_____    _____
_____

**3.**
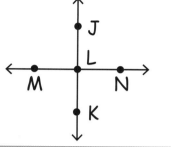
_____    _____

_____
_____

**4.** G      H
    Y      Z
_____    _____

_____

---

## Basic Terms

| | |
|---|---|
| A ● | This is a *point.* It marks an exact location. |
| B ●———● C | This is a *line.* This line is named $\overleftrightarrow{BC}$. |
| D ●———● E | This is a *ray.* It is part of a line that goes on forever in one direction. This ray is named $\overrightarrow{DE}$. |
| F | An *intersection* is the point where two lines cross. These lines cross at point F. |
| G ●———● H <br> I ●———● J | These are *parallel lines.* They are always the same distance apart so they never cross. These are named $\overleftrightarrow{GH} \parallel \overleftrightarrow{IJ}$. |
| 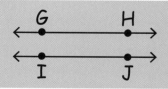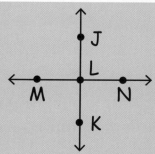 | These are *perpendicular lines.* They intersect to form right angles. These are named $\overleftrightarrow{JK} \perp \overleftrightarrow{MN}$. |

---

Lines, Angles, Shapes

# Draw It!

**1.** Draw a line segment.
Label it AB.

**3.** Draw a ray. Label it DE.

**2.** Draw parallel lines. Label
the lines MN and PR.

**4.** Draw perpendicular
lines. Label the lines WX
and YZ.

Lines, Angles, Shapes

Classify each angle as *right*, *acute*, or *obtuse*.

**1.** 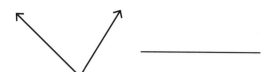 _____

**5.** 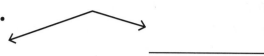 _____

**2.**  _____

**6.** 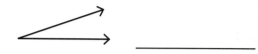 _____

**3.** 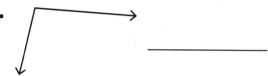 _____

**7.**  _____

**4.** 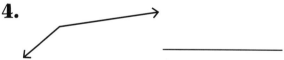 _____

**8.** 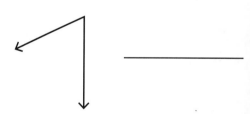 _____

**Lines, Angles, Shapes**

---

### Remember:

An angle is formed by two rays with a common end point called a *vertex*.

A *right angle* is exactly 90°.

An *acute angle* is less than 90°.

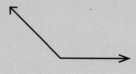

An *obtuse angle* is more than 90°.

# Answer the Question

Draw a straight line between the angles on the left and the type of angle on the right. Each line will go through at least one number. Write the corresponding letter on the line above the number. The letters will spell out the solution to the question.

A group of wolves is called a pack. What is a group of bears called?

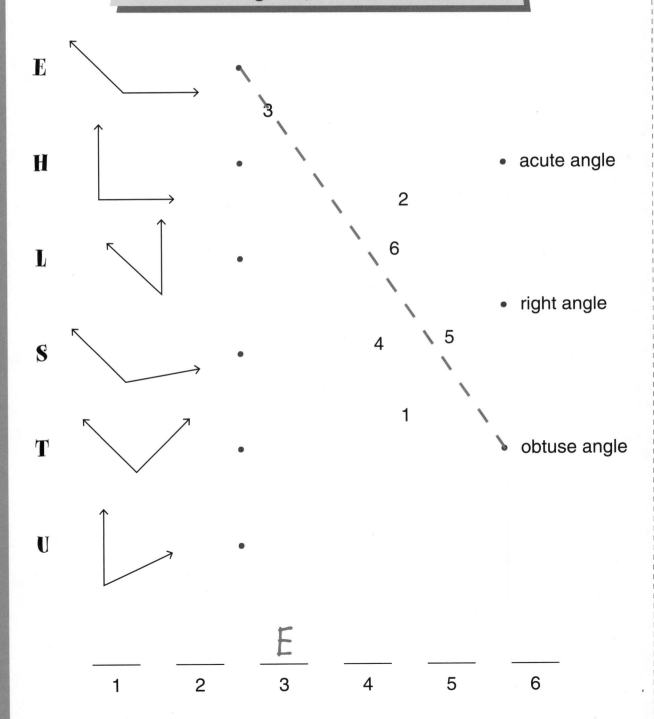

E

H

L

S

T

U

· acute angle

· right angle

· obtuse angle

3

2

6

4  5

1

___  ___  _E_  ___  ___  ___
 1    2    3    4    5    6

**Lines, Angles, Shapes**

**68**

Math • EMC 4550 • ©2005 by Evan-Moor Corp.

Note: The student will need a protractor
to complete pages 69 and 70.

# What's My Angle?

Using a protractor, measure each of the following angles to the nearest 5°.

**Skills:**

Measuring Angles Using a Protractor

**1.**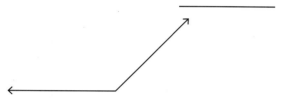

**5.**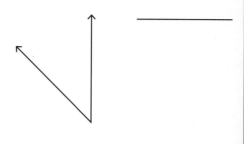

**2.**

**6.**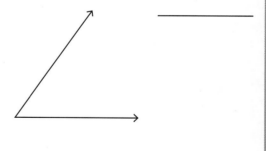

**3.**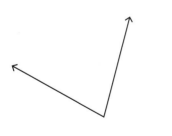

**7.**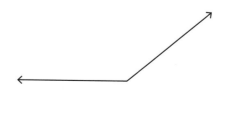

**4.**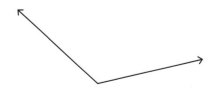

**8.**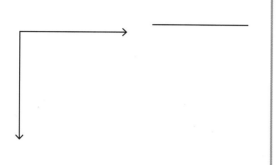

Lines, Angles, Shapes

©2005 by Evan-Moor Corp. • EMC 4550 • Math

UNIT 6

69

# What Can Be Right but Never Wrong?

Note: The student will need a protractor to complete pages 69 and 70.

**Skills:**

Measuring Angles Using a Protractor

To solve the riddle, measure each of the following angles with a protractor (to the nearest 10°). Then write the corresponding letter on the line above the angle measure. The letters will spell out the solution to the riddle.

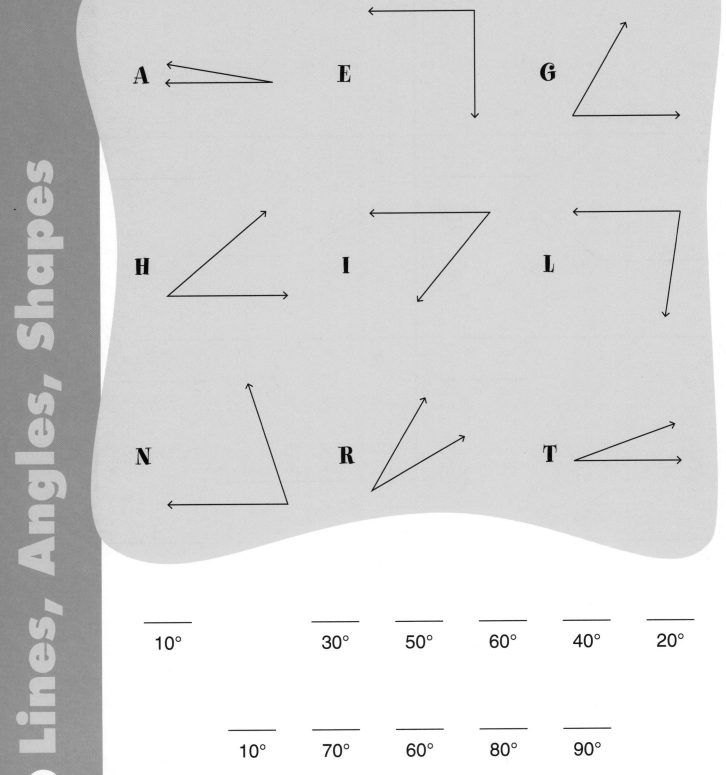

| ___ | | ___ | ___ | ___ | ___ | ___ |
|---|---|---|---|---|---|---|
| 10° | | 30° | 50° | 60° | 40° | 20° |

| ___ | ___ | ___ | ___ | ___ |
|---|---|---|---|---|
| 10° | 70° | 60° | 80° | 90° |

**Lines, Angles, Shapes**

# 3-Dimensional Figures

Complete the following chart by listing how many faces, edges, and vertices each of the given shapes has. Don't forget to count the faces, edges, and vertices on the backside that you can't see in the figure.

| Figure | Number of Faces | Number of Edges | Number of Vertices |
|---|---|---|---|
| 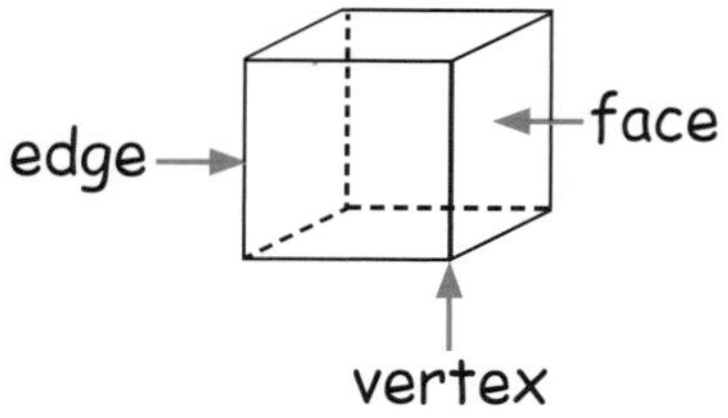 edge → face vertex | | | |
| 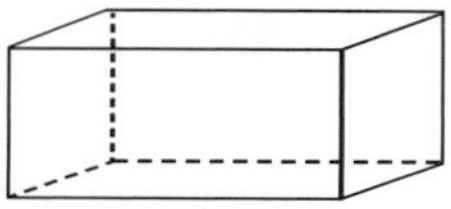 | | | |
| 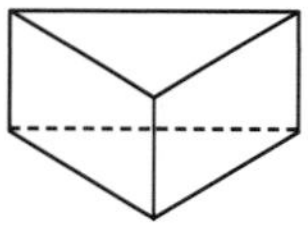 | | | |
| 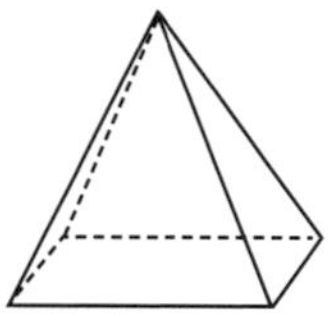 | | | |
| 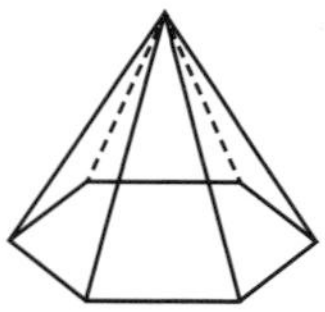 | | | |

# Tongue Twister

**Skills:**

Identifying Two-Dimensional Blueprints (Nets) of Three-Dimensional Figures

Look at each three-dimensional figure in the box. If you were to cut along each edge and lay the faces out flat, you would have a two-dimensional shape called a *net*. Write the corresponding letter for each three-dimensional figure above its net. The letters will spell out a tongue twister. Try to say it fast three times.

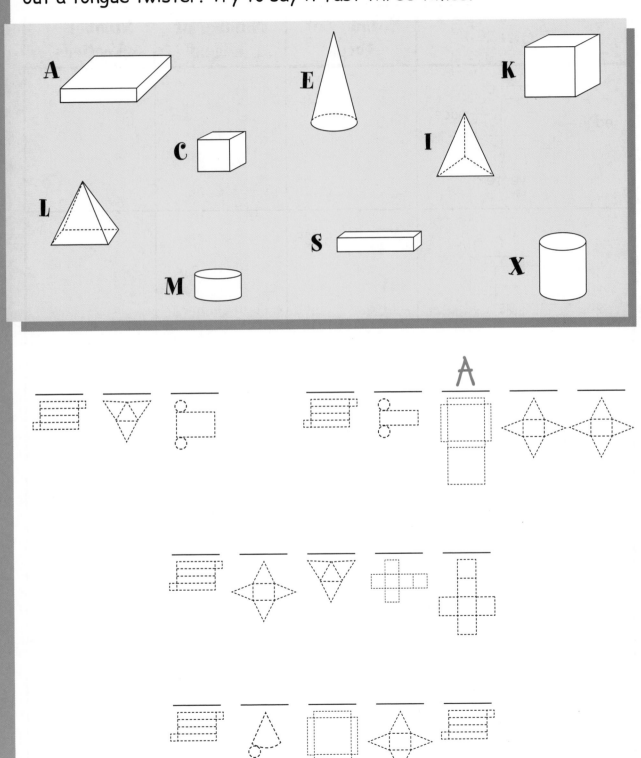

**Lines, Angles, Shapes**

72 UNIT 6

Math • EMC 4550 • ©2005 by Evan-Moor Corp.

For each of the following figures, draw the net. Remember that a net is the flat drawing as if you were to cut along the edges of the figure and lay the faces out flat. The first one has been drawn for you as an example. Also, notice that there are many different ways to draw a net.

**1.**

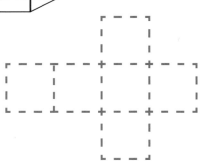

**4.**

**2.**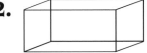

**5.**

**3.**

**6.**

Lines, Angles, Shapes

Skills:

Locating
and Plotting
Ordered
Pairs on a
Coordinate
Graph

# Mystery Shape

Plot the ordered pairs of numbers on the graph in the order in which they are listed, connecting them with straight lines. Start each new set of points with a new line. Remember: The first number moves backward or forward across (horizontally), and the second number moves up or down (vertically).

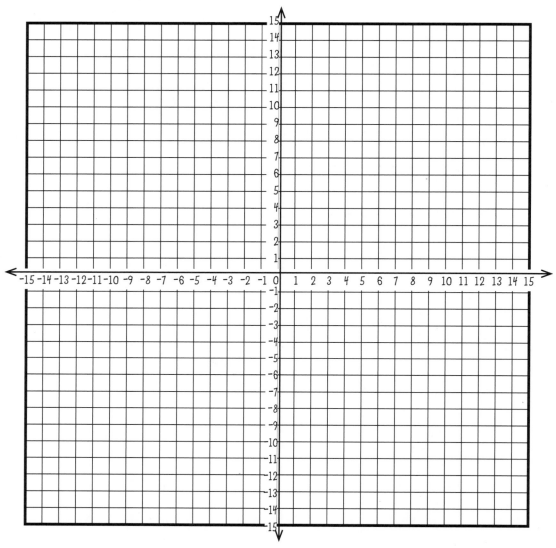

▸ (−11, −8) (10, −8) (10, 2) line ends

▸ (−8, −3) (−8, 7) (13, 7) line ends

▸ (−11, −8) (−8, −3) (13, −3) line ends

▸ (−11, 2) (−8, 7) line ends

▸ (10, −8) (13, −3) line ends

▸ (10, 2) (13, 7) line ends

▸ (13, −3) (13, 7) line ends

▸ (10, 2) (−11, 2) (−11, −8) line ends

# Name the Shape

Read the characteristics of a shape. Write each shape's name on the correct line.

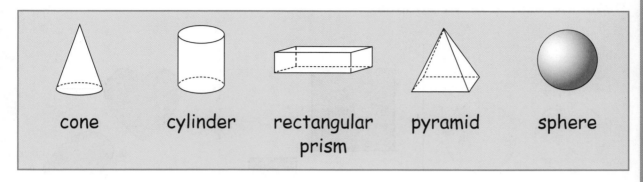

| cone | cylinder | rectangular prism | pyramid | sphere |

**Skills:**

Identifying Three-Dimensional Shapes

1. A 3-dimensional figure with two parallel and congruent circles as bases.   _____

2. A 3-dimensional figure with a circular base and one vertex.   _____

3. A 3-dimensional figure with two congruent parallel bases that are polygons.   _____

4. A 3-dimensional figure with a curved surface where all points are the same distance from a point called the *center*.   _____

5. A 3-dimensional figure whose base is a polygon and whose other faces are triangles that share a common vertex.   _____

> ### Remember:
>
> Congruent shapes are exactly the same shape and size.
>
> Parallel lines are the same distance apart at all times.
>
> Polygons are 2-dimensional (flat) shapes.

**Lines, Angles, Shapes**

# Similar or Congruent?

Congruent figures are the same size and shape. Similar figures are the same shape, but different sizes. Write **similar** or **congruent** to describe each pair of shapes.

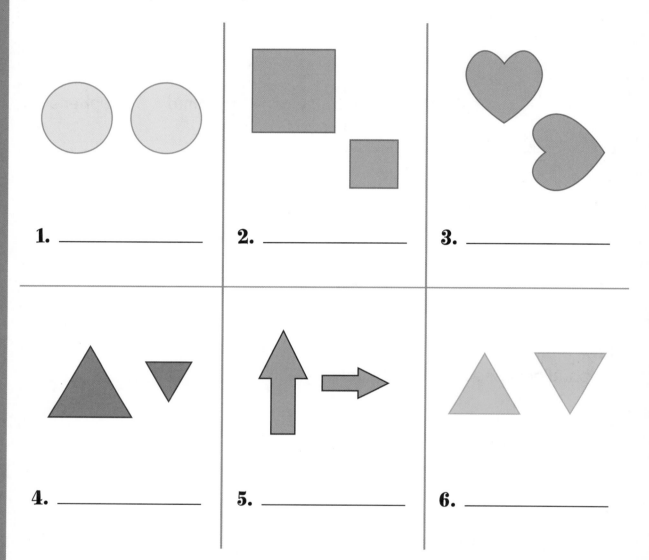

1. _____

2. _____

3. _____

4. _____

5. _____

6. _____

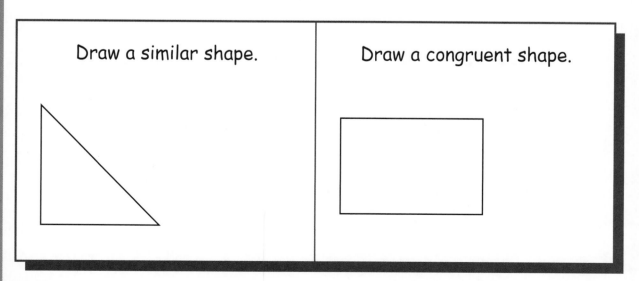

Draw a similar shape.

Draw a congruent shape.

**Lines, Angles, Shapes**

Note: Use this assessment after your child has completed through page 76.

Fill in the circle next to the correct answer.

**1.** What describes these lines?
- Ⓐ perpendicular
- Ⓑ ray
- Ⓒ point
- Ⓓ parallel

**2.** What describes these lines?
- Ⓐ perpendicular
- Ⓑ an obtuse angle
- Ⓒ point
- Ⓓ parallel

**3.** What type of angle is this?
- Ⓐ an acute angle
- Ⓑ ray
- Ⓒ a right angle
- Ⓓ a straight angle

**4.** What type of angle is this?
- Ⓐ an acute angle
- Ⓑ an obtuse angle
- Ⓒ a right angle
- Ⓓ a straight angle

**5.** What type of angle is this?
- Ⓐ an acute angle
- Ⓑ an obtuse angle
- Ⓒ a right angle
- Ⓓ a straight angle

**Use a protractor to measure the angles in numbers 6 and 7.**

**6.** What is the measure of this angle?
- Ⓐ 80°
- Ⓑ 85°
- Ⓒ 95°
- Ⓓ 145°

**7.** What is the measure of this angle?
- Ⓐ 150°
- Ⓑ 140°
- Ⓒ 95°
- Ⓓ 40°

**8.** Draw an angle that measures 45°.

**Use this figure for numbers 9 through 11.**

**9.** How many faces on a cube?
- Ⓐ 6     Ⓒ 10
- Ⓑ 8     Ⓓ 12

**10.** How many edges on a cube?
- Ⓐ 6     Ⓒ 10
- Ⓑ 8     Ⓓ 12

**11.** How many vertices on a cube?
- Ⓐ 6     Ⓒ 10
- Ⓑ 8     Ⓓ 12

**12.** Plot point **A** at (−2, 1) and point **B** at (0, −2) on this graph.

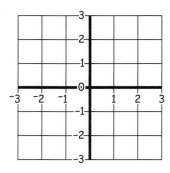

# Shopping for Shoes

**Skills:**

Comparing Values Using <, >, =

Help Angie find the way to Shoes for Less. Decide if each inequality is true (T) or false (F). Then go in the direction of the correct arrow. Continue through the maze until you come to Shoes for Less.

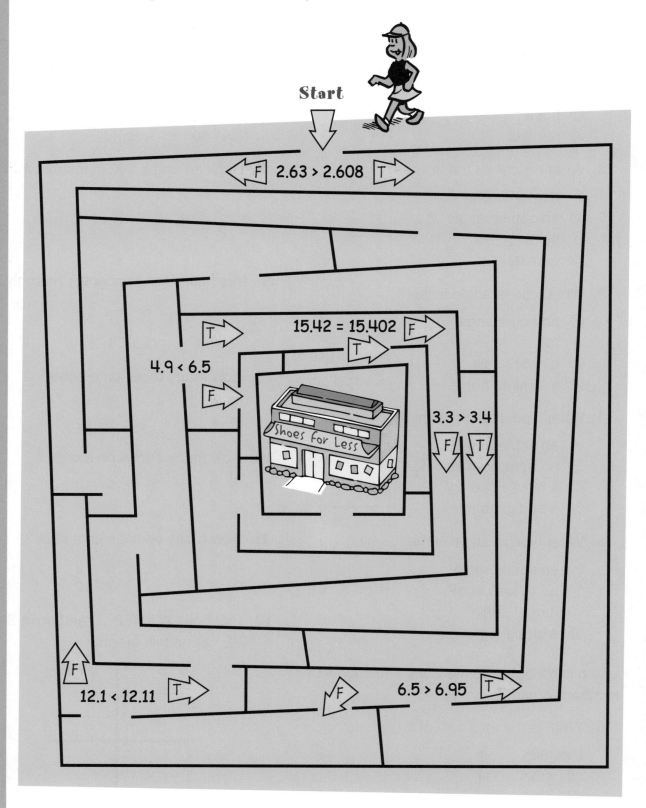

Start

F  2.63 > 2.608  T

T

15.42 = 15.402  F

T

4.9 < 6.5

F

3.3 > 3.4

F   T

F

12.1 < 12.11  T

F   6.5 > 6.95  T

At the Mall

# Percents

**What is 50% of each number?**

**1.** 6 _____

**2.** 50 _____

**3.** 28 _____

**4.** 300 _____

**What is 25% of each number?**

**5.** 6 _____

**6.** 50 _____

**7.** 28 _____

**8.** 300 _____

**What is 40% of each number?**

**9.** 6 _____

**10.** 50 _____

**11.** 28 _____

**12.** 300 _____

**What is 75% of each number?**

**13.** 6 _____

**14.** 50 _____

**15.** 28 _____

**16.** 300 _____

**At the Mall**

### Remember:

To find a percent of a number, multiply the number by the percent written in its decimal form.

| 25% of 8 | 10% of 35 |
|---|---|
| $0.25 \times 8 = 2$ | $0.10 \times 35 = 3.5$ |

# On Sale

Solve each problem.

1. Julia was shopping at a store that advertised 50% off everything. She found a new CD player originally priced at $76. What was the sale price?

   _____

2. Roberto bought a new shirt that was 25% off. The original price was $60. How much did he save?

   _____

3. Elena was shopping for a new bathing suit. She found one she really liked. It was for sale at 40% off. In order to figure out how much the discount was, she needed to convert the percent into a decimal. What is 40% as a decimal?

   _____

   If the bathing suit cost $36 and was 40% off, how much did Elena pay for it?

   _____

4. Eddie found a jersey he really liked that was $\frac{1}{5}$ off. At another store, he found the same jersey listed at the same original price, but it was discounted 15% off.

   If the jersey cost $20 and was $\frac{1}{5}$ off, how much would Eddie pay for it?

   _____

   If the jersey cost $20 and was 15% off, how much would Eddie pay for it?

   _____

5. Tax for Northglenn City is calculated at 6.5%. Carlos is at a convenience store with his mom and needs to convert the percent to a decimal to input it on his calculator. What decimal number should he use?

   _____

At the Mall

The owners of the mall have asked that each shop be redecorated. The Cut and Style Shop wants to paint a yellow stripe around the inside walls of the building. The diagram shows the floor plan for the shop.

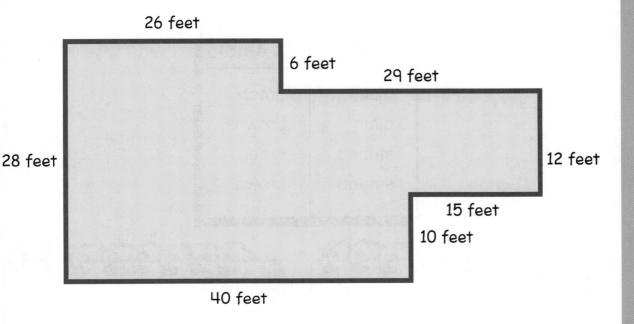

26 feet

6 feet

29 feet

28 feet

12 feet

15 feet

10 feet

40 feet

**1.** How long will the yellow stripe be?

_____

**2.** Is there a shorter way to solve this problem without adding up all of the dimensions on the diagram?

_____

_____

_____

# What Shall I Buy?

This organized list shows the number of choices that can be created from two pairs of pants (plain and striped) and two colors of shirts (green and brown). Each row lists one possible outfit. There are a total of four different outfits in this organized list. Make an organized list for each of the following:

| Design | Color |
|---------|--------|
| plain | green |
| plain | brown |
| striped | green |
| striped | brown |

1. jackets in three sizes (small, medium, large) and two colors (blue and yellow)

2. shirts in four designs (striped, polka-dots, plain, checkered) and three colors (red, purple, orange)

At the Mall

**Skills:**

Calculating
Least Common
Multiple (LCM)
for up to Three
Numbers Less
Than 25

**What did the bird buy at the mall?**

To solve the riddle, find the Least Common Multiple (LCM) for each set of numbers. Then write the corresponding letter on the line above the LCM. The letters will spell out the solution to the riddle.

**A** LCM of 2 and 4 = _____

**E** LCM of 5 and 6 = _____

**E** LCM of 3 and 4 = _____

**E** LCM of 4 and 5 = _____

**E** LCM of 6 and 9 = _____

**S** LCM of 5 and 3 = _____

**T** LCM of 7 and 3 = _____

**T** LCM of 22 and 4 = _____

**T** LCM of 16 and 3 = _____

**W** LCM of 6 and 8 = _____

**W** LCM of 10 and 8 = _____

| ___ | ___ | ___ | ___ | ___ | ___ |
|---|---|---|---|---|---|
| 4 | 15 | 40 | 12 | 30 | 44 |

| ___ | ___ | ___ | ___ | ___ |
|---|---|---|---|---|
| 21 | 24 | 20 | 18 | 48 |

**Remember:**

The least common multiple (LCM) of two or more numbers is the smallest multiple that occurs for each number being compared.

The LCM of 4 and 5 is 20.

The LCM of 2, 3, and 4 is 12.

**At the Mall**

# Tongue Twister

**Skills:**

Adding and Subtracting Fractions (Mixed Numbers & Unlike Denominators)

To find the tongue twister, complete each of the following problems. Then write the corresponding letter on the line in front of each problem. Read the letters from top to bottom. Try to say it quickly five times.

**S**    $2\frac{1}{4} + 3\frac{1}{2} =$ $5\frac{3}{4}$

____    $2\frac{2}{3} + 1\frac{2}{3} =$ _____

____    $8\frac{1}{3} - 3\frac{1}{12} =$ _____

____    $7\frac{1}{3} - 2 =$ _____

____    $2\frac{1}{3} + 3\frac{5}{12} =$ _____

____    $2\frac{7}{12} + 1\frac{3}{4} =$ _____

____    $9\frac{3}{4} - 4\frac{1}{2} =$ _____

____    $6\frac{1}{3} - 1\frac{5}{6} =$ _____

| | |
|---|---|
| $5\frac{1}{3}$ | **E** |
| $4\frac{1}{2}$ | **P** |
| $5\frac{3}{4}$ | **S** |
| $4\frac{1}{3}$ | **H** |
| $5\frac{1}{4}$ | **O** |

## Remember:

To add or subtract mixed numbers with different denominators:

1. Change the mixed numbers to improper fractions.

2. Find the least common multiple (LCM) for each denominator.

3. Convert the fractions.

4. Then add or subtract.

5. Reduce the answer to the simplest terms.

Example:
$2\frac{2}{3} + 1\frac{3}{4} =$ ___

1. $2\frac{2}{3} = \frac{8}{3}$, $1\frac{3}{4} = \frac{7}{4}$

2. Least common multiple is 12.

3. $\frac{8}{3} = \frac{32}{12}$, $\frac{7}{4} = \frac{21}{12}$

4. $\frac{32}{12} + \frac{21}{12} = \frac{53}{12}$

5. $\frac{53}{12} = 4\frac{5}{12}$

**At the Mall**

There were 200 customers at the Soda Shop last Saturday. Mrs. McCool kept track of the number of people that bought each type of soda she sold. Here are the results:

| Chocolate: | 70 customers | Root Beer: | 50 customers |
| Strawberry: | 34 customers | Vanilla: | 16 customers |
| Orange: | 10 customers | Cherry: | 20 customers |

Use the information to complete the circle graph below. Make a key and color each section a different color. Be sure the colors on your key match the data and your graph.

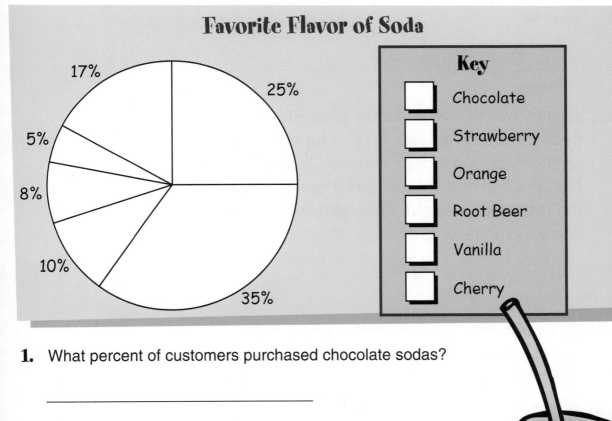

### Favorite Flavor of Soda

17%
25%
5%
8%
10%
35%

**Key**

☐ Chocolate

☐ Strawberry

☐ Orange

☐ Root Beer

☐ Vanilla

☐ Cherry

1. What percent of customers purchased chocolate sodas?

_____

2. What is the difference in the largest percent and the smallest percent shown on the graph?

_____

3. What is the total percentage shown on the graph?

_____

At the Mall

# Better Buy

Skills:

Compare
Values Using
<, >, and =

Calculate
with Whole
Numbers,
Fractions, and
Percents

In each of the following situations, determine which one is the cheaper purchase. Write the values from the problem in a math sentence using the <, >, and = symbols.

$$\$21 < \$54$$
$$\$12 > \$9$$
$$\$17 = \$17$$

**1.** Ralph saw two different CD players. One was originally priced at $75 and was $\frac{1}{4}$ off. The other one was originally priced at $90 and was 30% off. Find the final price of each CD player. Then list them in order from the cheapest to the most expensive using the correct inequality symbol.

_____

**2.** Ali saw two different videos. One was originally priced at $30 and was $\frac{1}{5}$ off. The other was originally priced at $20 and was $\frac{1}{10}$ off. Find the final price of each video. List them in order from the most expensive to the cheapest using the correct inequality symbol.

_____

**3.** Jan, Max, and Jacob each bought a new jacket. Jan's was originally priced at $80 and was 15% off. Max's was originally price at $136 and was $\frac{1}{2}$ off. Jacob's was originally priced at $90 and was 1% off. Find the final price of each jacket. Which two cost the same?

_____

Write the two prices using the correct symbol.

_____

At the Mall

# Book Costs

Skills:

Adding and
Subtracting
Decimals

1. Georgia is buying three books. They cost $14.00, $15.95, and $17.50. What is the total cost of the three books?

_____

If Georgia paid for the books with three $20 bills, how much change would she get back?

_____

2. Sally bought three books at the store yesterday, one for herself and two for her mother. The total bill came to $45.90 prior to tax. The book that Sally bought for herself cost $17.95. What was the total for the two books she bought for her mother?

_____

3. Walker Book Store can purchase a book for $12.93 and then sell the same book for $14.50. How much profit do they make from the sale of this book?

_____

How much profit would Walker Book Store make if 10 books were sold?

_____

4. Timothy bought four books and one journal. The books cost $4.95, $5.75, $10.25, and $14.99. The total of the five items was $44.39. How much was the journal?

_____

5. Patricia bought a book at the store for a certain amount. She got $2.00 from her mom to buy the book, $3.25 from her dad, and $4.00 from her older sister. Patricia had to kick in the last $2.49. How much did the book cost?

_____

©2005 by Evan-Moor Corp. • EMC 4550 • Math

At the Mall

UNIT 7      87

# At the Mall

Complete this logic puzzle to determine which shop each person went to first.

| | Video Store | Games Store | Shoe Store | Book Store | Pet Shop | Sandwich Nook |
|---|---|---|---|---|---|---|
| Alicia | | | | | | |
| Ann | | | | | | |
| Geraldo | | | | | | |
| Rachel | | | | | | |
| Raul | | | | | | |
| Tim | | | | | | |

## Clues

★ Each person went to a different store first.

★ None of the girls went to the Sandwich Nook first.

★ Ann went to the Book Store first.

★ The oldest boy went to the Games Store first, and the youngest girl went to the Shoe Store first.

★ Alicia did not go to the Pet Store first.

★ Raul did not go to the Sandwich Nook first.

★ Geraldo went to the Games Store first.

★ A girl went to the Pet Shop first.

### Remember:

Use the directions on page 24 if you've forgotten how to complete a logic puzzle.

**TEST YOUR SKILLS**

Fill in the circle next to the correct answer. If possible, simplify each fraction.

**1.** $\frac{3}{5} + \frac{1}{5} =$ _____

    Ⓐ $\frac{4}{10}$       Ⓒ $\frac{4}{5}$

    Ⓑ $\frac{2}{5}$       Ⓓ $\frac{3}{5}$

**2.** $5\frac{3}{4} + 4\frac{1}{2} =$ _____

    Ⓐ $9\frac{1}{4}$       Ⓒ $9\frac{2}{3}$

    Ⓑ $9\frac{4}{6}$       Ⓓ $10\frac{1}{4}$

**3.** $\frac{6}{7} - \frac{5}{7} =$ _____

    Ⓐ $\frac{1}{7}$       Ⓒ $\frac{2}{7}$

    Ⓑ $1$       Ⓓ $\frac{11}{7}$

**4.** Jimmy started with a string that was $25\frac{1}{3}$ feet long. He cut off a piece that was $6\frac{3}{4}$ feet long to give to his friend. How much string does Jimmy have left?

_____

**5.** What is 75% of 32?

    Ⓐ 75       Ⓒ 25

    Ⓑ 24       Ⓓ 16

**6.** Tim found a jacket that was 25% off. The original price was $45.00. What was the sale price?

    Ⓐ $65.00       Ⓒ $20.25

    Ⓑ $11.00       Ⓓ $33.75

**7.** Which math sentence is true?

    Ⓐ 5.4 > 5.51       Ⓒ 3.52 > 3.49

    Ⓑ 2.49 > 2.5       Ⓓ 6.12 > 6.23

**8.** Which symbol could complete the following?

         4.7 ☐ 4.24

    Ⓐ <       Ⓒ >

    Ⓑ =       Ⓓ all of the above

**9.** What is the LCM (least common multiple) of 3 and 4?

    Ⓐ 12       Ⓒ 4

    Ⓑ 3       Ⓓ 1

**10.** What is the LCM of 9 and 12?

    Ⓐ 72       Ⓒ 1

    Ⓑ 3       Ⓓ 36

**11.** Draw an organized list to show all the possible combinations of three shirts (red, blue, and green) and two pants (blue and black).

**12.** If there were 40 children surveyed, about how many more children liked orange compared to grape?

    Ⓐ 1

    Ⓑ 5

    Ⓒ 10

    Ⓓ 15

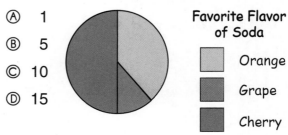

Favorite Flavor of Soda

Orange
Grape
Cherry

# Missing Numbers

**Skills:**

Solving Equations with One Variable

Solve each of the following equations. Show all of your work.

| | |
|---|---|
| Add the same value to each side.<br><br>$x - 6 = 3$<br>$x - 6 + 6 = 3 + 6$<br>$x = 9$ | Multiply both sides by the same number.<br><br>$y \div 2 = 3$<br>$y \div 2 \times 2 = 3 \times 2$<br>$y = 6$ |
| Or subtract the same value from each side.<br><br>$x + 2 = 7$<br>$x + 2 - 2 = 7 - 2$<br>$x = 5$ | Or divide both sides by the same number.<br><br>$2y = 8$<br>$2y \div 2 = 8 \div 2$<br>$y = 4$ |

**1.** $x + 4 = 5$     $x =$ _____

**2.** $x + 8 = 12$     $x =$ _____

**3.** $x + 5 = 5,$     $x =$ _____

**4.** $x + 2 = 11$     $x =$ _____

**5.** $x + 6 = 21$     $x =$ _____

**6.** $x - 5 = 8$     $x =$ _____

**7.** $x - 4 = 13$     $x =$ _____

**8.** $x - 9 = 13$     $x =$ _____

**9.** $x - 5 = 26$     $x =$ _____

**10.** $6y = 24$     $y =$ _____

**11.** $3y = 18$     $y =$ _____

**12.** $9y = 54$     $y =$ _____

**13.** $12y = 48$     $y =$ _____

**14.** $3y = 33$     $y =$ _____

**15.** $y \div 7 = 2$   $y =$ _____

**16.** $y \div 3 = 9$   $y =$ _____

**17.** $y \div 1 = 7$   $y =$ _____

**18.** $y \div 8 = 6$   $y =$ _____

Math Recipes

# Times Myself

exponent
|
$2^2$
|
base

The large number is called a *base*.
The small number is called an
*exponent*. It shows how many
times the base is used as a factor.

$5^2$ is read as "five squared."
It tells you to multiply 5 by itself two times.
$5 \times 5 = 25$

$4^3$ is read 4 "cubed."
It tells you to multiply 4 by itself three times.
$4 \times 4 \times 4 = 64$

$2^5$ is read as "2 to the fifth power."
It tells you to multiply 2 by itself five times.
$2 \times 2 \times 2 \times 2 \times 2 = 32$

**Math Recipes**

Solve these problems using exponents:

**1.** $4^2 =$ _____

**2.** $2^3 =$ _____

**3.** $3^5 =$ _____

**4.** $8^2 =$ _____

**5.** $4^5 =$ _____

**6.** $5^3 =$ _____

Solve these equations using exponents:

**7.** $2^2 + 3^3 =$ _____

**8.** $3^5 - 2^3 =$ _____

**9.** $5^2 \times 3^3 =$ _____

**10.** $3^3 \div 3^2 =$ _____

# Perimeters, Please

**Perimeter** is the distance around a shape. Find the perimeter (P) of each shape below by adding together the lengths of each side.

**1.**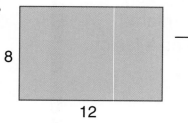

**2.**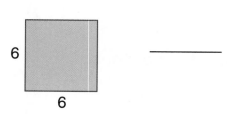

**3.**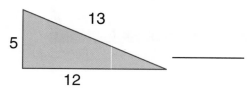

**4.**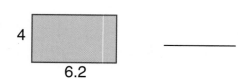

**5.**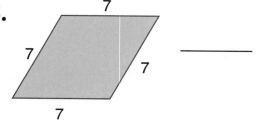

**6.**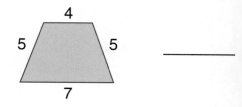

**7.**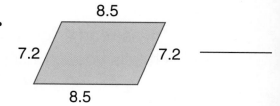

**8.**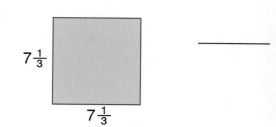

**9.**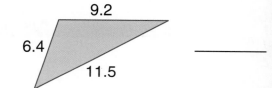

**10.**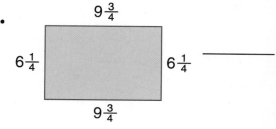

Math • EMC 4550 • ©2005 by Evan-Moor Corp.

# Perimeter Formulas

Use the formula to find the perimeter of each shape. Show each step.

| Shape | Formula | Perimeter |
|---|---|---|
| 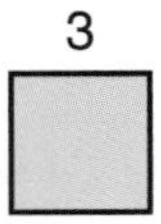 3<br>□<br>square | $P = 4 \times s$ | $P = 4 \times$ _____<br><br>$P =$ _____ |
| 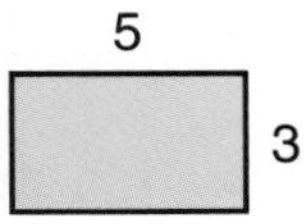 5<br>▭ 3<br>rectangle | $P = (2 \times w) + (2 \times l)$ | $P = (2 \times$ _____$) + (2 \times$ _____$)$<br><br>$P =$ _____ $+$ _____<br><br>$P =$ _____ |
| 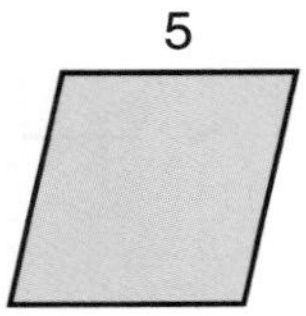 5<br>▱<br>rhombus | $P = 4 \times s$ | $P = 4 \times$ _____<br><br>$P =$ _____ |
| 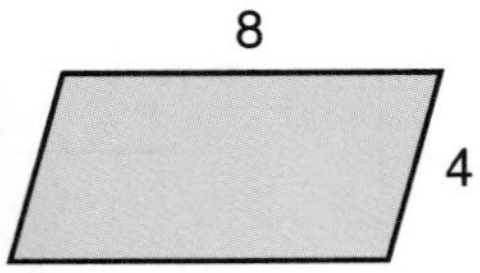 8<br>▱ 4<br>parallelogram | $P = (2 \times w) + (2 \times l)$ | $P = (2 \times$ _____$) + (2 \times$ _____$)$<br><br>$P =$ _____ $+$ _____<br><br>$P =$ _____ |
| 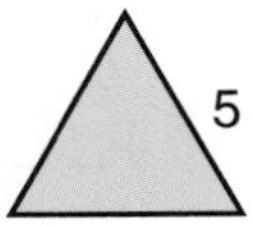 △ 5<br>equilateral triangle | $P = 3 \times s$ | $P = 3 \times$ _____<br><br>$P =$ _____ |

**Remember:**

$P$ = perimeter     $w$ = width
$s$ = side         $l$ = length

Math Recipes

# Give Me Your Area

**Area** is the size of a flat surface in square units. Find the area
of each shape.

**1.**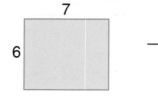
7
6
_____

**2.**
4
4
_____

**3.**
8
3
_____

**4.**
5
8
_____

**5.**
12
5
_____

**6.**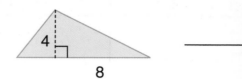
4
8
_____

**7.**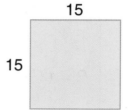
15
15
_____

**8.**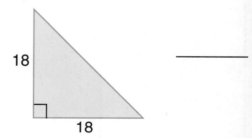
18
18
_____

**9.**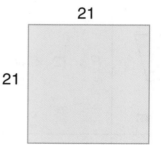
21
21
_____

**10.**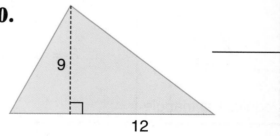
9
12
_____

**Remember:**

Find the area of a square or rectangle by multiplying height times the base. Find
the area of a triangle by multiplying the height by the base and dividing by 2.

Math • EMC 4550 • ©2005 by Evan-Moor Corp.

Math Recipes

Julie's older sister is working a geometry homework problem. She is finding the area of a trapezoid.

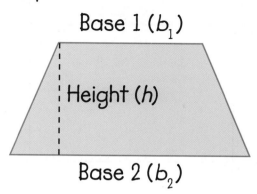

Base 1 ($b_1$)

Height ($h$)

Base 2 ($b_2$)

Her sister explains that the formula for finding the area of the trapezoid is:

$$A = \tfrac{1}{2} \times (b_1 + b_2) \times h$$

This formula means that you first add the lengths of the two bases (since they are in parentheses) and then multiply that sum by $\frac{1}{2}$. Then you multiply the result by the height. This gives you the area of the trapezoid.

**Use this formula and follow the order of operations to complete the table below for the area of three different trapezoids.**

|  | Base 1 | Base 2 | Height | Area |
|---|---|---|---|---|
| Trapezoid 1 | 4 inches | 6 inches | 3 inches | |
| Trapezoid 2 | 5 inches | 8 inches | 4 inches | |
| Trapezoid 3 | 10 inches | 15 inches | 6 inches | |

**Remember:**

If you need a reminder for how to do order of operations, refer to page 9.

Math Recipes

# My Area Is...

Use the formula to find the area of each shape. Show each step.

| Shape | Formula | Area |
|---|---|---|
| 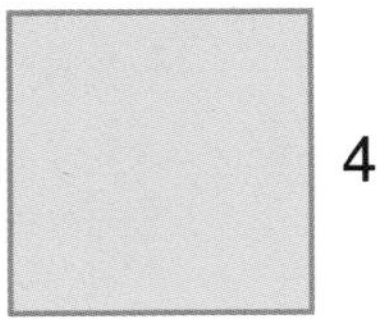 <br> square | $A = s^2$ | $A = $ _____ × _____ <br><br> $A = $ _____ square units |
| 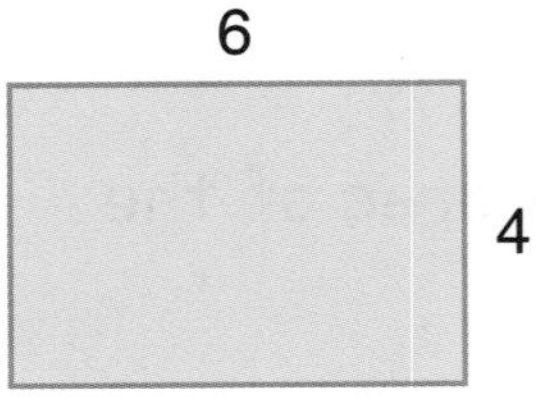 <br> rectangle | $A = b \times h$ | $A = $ _____ × _____ <br><br> $A = $ _____ square units |
| 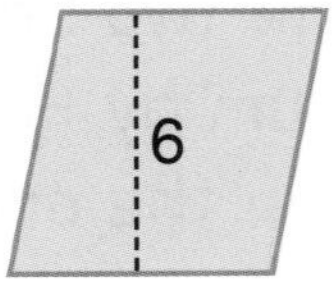 <br> rhombus | $A = b \times h$ | $A = $ _____ × _____ <br><br> $A = $ _____ square units |
| 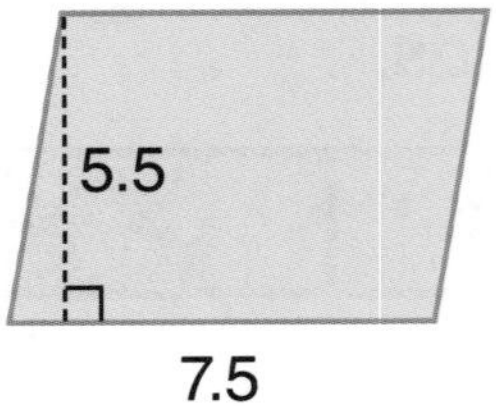 <br> parallelogram | $A = b \times h$ | $A = $ _____ × _____ <br><br> $A = $ _____ square units |
| 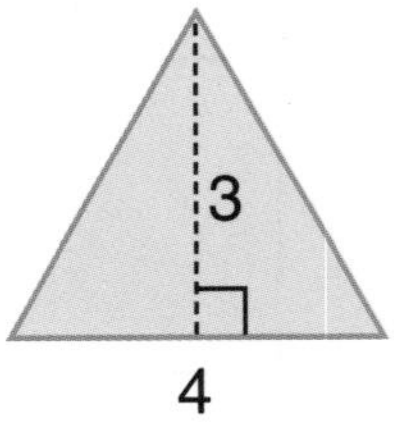 <br> equilateral triangle | $A = \dfrac{b \times h}{2}$ | $A = \dfrac{\Box \times \Box}{2}$ <br><br> $A = $ _____ square units |

## Remember:

$A$ = area
$s$ = side
$b$ = base
$h$ = height

side

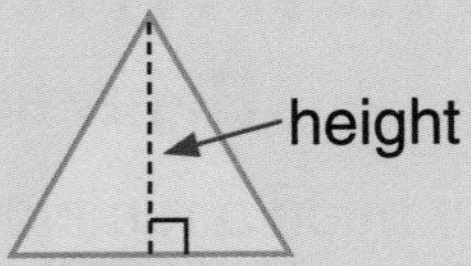

height
base

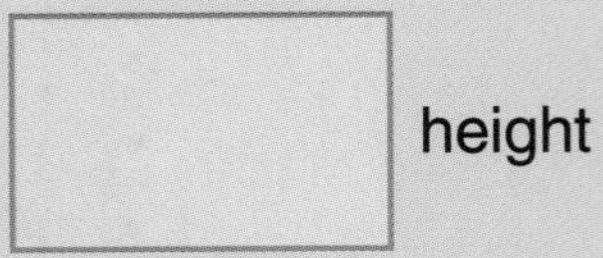

height
base

Math Recipes

**Volume** is the amount of space contained inside a three-dimensional shape. Find the volume of each shape below by multiplying length by height by width.

$$\boxed{\begin{array}{c} \text{Volume} = \text{length} \times \text{height} \times \text{width} \\ V = l \times h \times w \end{array}}$$

**1.**

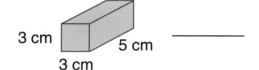

3 cm     5 cm
3 cm

_____

**4.**

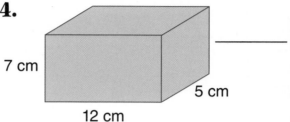

7 cm     5 cm
12 cm

_____

**2.**

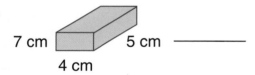

7 cm     5 cm
4 cm

_____

**5.**

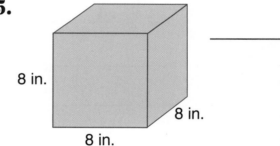

8 in.     8 in.
8 in.

_____

**3.**

2 cm     2 cm
2 cm

_____

**6.**

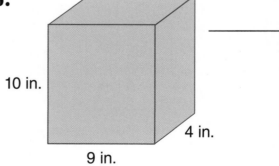

10 in.     4 in.
9 in.

_____

Math Recipes

# How Large Is It?

**Skills:**

Calculating
Perimeter, Area,
and Volume

Solve these problems.

**1.** Given these two shapes, tell which has a larger perimeter and why.

6 in.

**A**

4 in.

**B**

_____

_____

_____

**2.** Given these two shapes, tell which has a larger area and why.

5 in.

2 in.

**A**

4 in.

3 in.

**B**

_____

_____

_____

**3.** Given these two boxes, tell which has a larger volume and why.

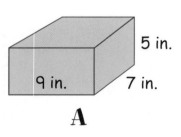

5 in.

9 in.     7 in.

**A**

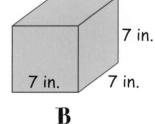

7 in.

7 in.     7 in.

**B**

_____

_____

_____

Math Recipes

# Area of a Circle

Find the area of each of the following circles:

**Skills:**

Finding the
Area of a Circle

**1.**  radius = 3 in.

$A = \pi \times r^2$    <u>28.26 in.$^2$</u>
$A = 3.14 \times 3 \times 3$
$A = 28.26$ in.$^2$

**6.** 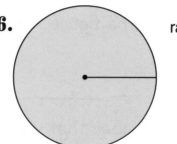 radius = 10 in.
_____

**2.**  radius = 4 in.
_____

**7.**  diameter = 4 cm
_____

**3.**  radius = 6 cm
_____

**8.**  diameter = 10 in.
_____

**4.**  radius = 7 cm
_____

**9.**  diameter = 16 cm
_____

**5.** 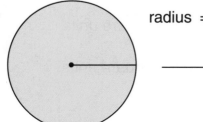 radius = 9 in.
_____

**10.**  diameter = 9 in.
_____

Math Recipes

# A Riddle

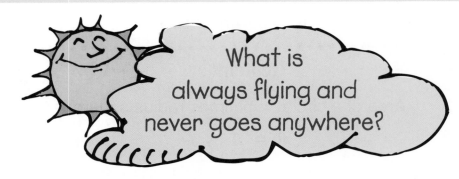

What is always flying and never goes anywhere?

To solve the riddle, find the area of each circle below. After you have computed each area, write the letter that corresponds to the area on the line below the figure. The letters spell out the solution to the riddle.

Remember that you can use the following formula to find the area of a circle:

Area of a circle = pi times radius squared

$$A = \pi \times r^2$$

Use 3.14 as the value of pi for these problems.

 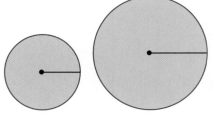 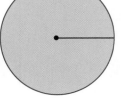 

| radius = 2 | radius = 4 | radius = 6 | diameter = 4 | radius = 5 |

___        ___        ___        ___        ___

**A**  12.56 square units     **L**  113.04 square units

**B**  28.26 square units     **M**  153.86 square units

**F**  50.24 square units     **S**  200.96 square units

**G**  78.5 square units

Math Recipes

# Circumference of a Circle

Find the circumference (distance around) each circle.

## Use these formulas:

If you know the diameter, use

$$C = \pi \times d$$

Circumference = pi times diameter

If you know the radius, use

$$C = 2\pi \times r$$

Circumference = 2 times pi times radius

Use 3.14 as the value of pi for these problems.

    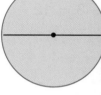 

| $r = 8$ | $r = 4$ | $r = 2$ | $d = 12$ | $r = 10$ | $d = 22$ |

$C = 2 \times \pi \times r$
$C = 2 \times 3.14 \times 8$
$C = 50.24$

**1.** _____  **2.** _____  **3.** _____  **4.** _____  **5.** _____  **6.** _____

     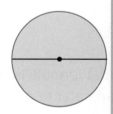

| $r = 7$ | $r = 3$ | $r = 9$ | $d = 14$ | $r = 5$ | $d = 10$ |

**7.** _____  **8.** _____  **9.** _____  **10.** _____  **11.** _____  **12.** _____

## Remember:

circumference

diameter

radius

Math Recipes

Fill in the circle next to the correct answer.

**1.** $x - 7 = 23$

   Ⓐ $x = 7$      Ⓒ $x = 23$

   Ⓑ $x = 16$    Ⓓ $x = 30$

**2.** $8y = 24$

   Ⓐ $y = 2$      Ⓒ $y = 24$

   Ⓑ $y = 3$      Ⓓ $y = 192$

**3.** $x \div 3 = 12$

   Ⓐ $x = 1$      Ⓒ $x = 12$

   Ⓑ $x = 4$      Ⓓ $x = 36$

**4.** $3^2 = $ _____

   Ⓐ 6         Ⓒ 5

   Ⓑ 9         Ⓓ 15

**5.** $2^3 = $ _____

   Ⓐ 2         Ⓒ 6

   Ⓑ 4         Ⓓ 8

**6.** What formula is used to figure the perimeter of a flat shape?

   Ⓐ length × height × width

   Ⓑ $3.14 \times r^2$

   Ⓒ 2 × width + 2 × length

   Ⓓ length × height

**7.** What formula is used to figure the area of a square or rectangle?

   Ⓐ length × height × width

   Ⓑ $3.14 \times r^2$

   Ⓒ 2 × width + 2 × length

   Ⓓ length × height

**8.** What formula is used to figure the volume of a cube or rectangular prism?

   Ⓐ length × height × width

   Ⓑ $3.14 \times r^2$

   Ⓒ 2 × width + 2 × length

   Ⓓ length × height

**9.** What is the perimeter of this triangle?

   Ⓐ 14

   Ⓑ 9    

   Ⓒ 8

   Ⓓ 54

**10.** What is the area of this square?

   Ⓐ 16 square units

   Ⓑ 15 square units

   Ⓒ 8 square units   

   Ⓓ 7.5 square units

**11.** What is the volume of this cube?

   Ⓐ 25 cubic centimeters

   Ⓑ 125 cubic centimeters

   Ⓒ 100 cubic centimeters   

   Ⓓ 30 cubic centimeters

**12.** What is the area of this circle?

   Ⓐ 78.5 square units

   Ⓑ 15.7 square units

   Ⓒ 31.4 square units   

   Ⓓ 69 square units

# It's a Fact

Hawai'i was the 50th state admitted to the United States of America. In fact, it was the last state. To find the capital city of Hawai'i, solve these problems. Then write the corresponding letter in the box above the answer. The letters will spell out the capital of Hawai'i.

**Skills:**

Adding
Negative
and Positive
Numbers

**H** $^-6 + {}^+9 =$ _____

**L** $^+9 + {}^-2 =$ _____

**L** $^-3 + {}^-12 =$ _____

**N** $^-4 + {}^-8 =$ _____

**O** $^+7 + {}^-7 =$ _____

**O** $^-6 + {}^-4 =$ _____

**U** $^-8 + {}^+2 =$ _____

**U** $^+11 + {}^-6 =$ _____

| | | | | | | | |
|---|---|---|---|---|---|---|---|
| +3 | ⁻10 | ⁻12 | 0 | +7 | ⁻6 | ⁻15 | +5 |

## Remember:

To add two numbers with the **same** sign:
  • Add the numbers together and use the common sign.

$$^-2 + {}^-4 = {}^-6$$

To add two numbers with **different** signs:
  • Subtract the smaller number from the larger number.
  • Use the sign of the larger number for the answer.

$$^-6 + {}^+2 = {}^-4$$

Aloha

©2005 by Evan-Moor Corp. • EMC 4550 • Math

UNIT 9

**103**

# Ordering Mixed Numbers

Plot each of the following points on the number line. Label each point with the corresponding letter. The letters will spell out the Hawaiian name for the state flower (a type of hibiscus).

| | |
|---|---|
| $4\frac{1}{3}$ | U |
| 7.9 | A |
| $5\frac{1}{10}$ | A |
| 11.4 | L |
| 8.5 | L |
| 3.75 | P |
| $9\frac{1}{2}$ | O |
| 10.5 | A |
| 12.2 | O |

**Aloha**

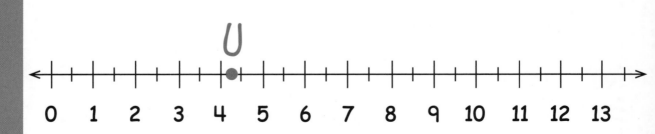

# The Hawaiian Islands

The chart shows information about the six largest Hawaiian islands. Use the information to complete the task.

| Island | Area | Coastline |
|---|---|---|
| Hawai'i | 4,028 square miles | 266 miles |
| Kauai | 552.3 square miles | 90 miles |
| Maui | 727.3 square miles | 120 miles |
| Molokai | 260.9 square miles | 88 miles |
| Lanai | 141 square miles | 47 miles |
| Oahu | 608 square miles | 141 miles |

**1.** Arrange the islands in order from smallest to largest area.

__________ __________ __________ __________ __________ __________

**2.** Arrange the islands in order from longest to shortest coastline.

__________ __________ __________ __________ __________ __________

**3.** Is the order of islands the same in both lists?

______________________________

Explain why or why not.

________________________________________________________

________________________________________________________

**Skills:**

Organizing Numbers in Numerical Order

Aloha

# Vacation Expenses

Use the information on the list below to answer the questions.

| | |
|---|---|
| $ 450.83 | Airfare |
| $ 400.62 | Hotel |
| $ 135.00 | Car Rental |
| $ 39.80 | Souvenirs |
| $ 150.00 | Scuba Diving & Surfing |
| $ 220.00 | Meals |
| $ 40.75 | Entrance Fees |

**1.** How much did Ms. Boomer spend on her Hawaiian vacation?

_____

**2.** Ms. Boomer saved $125.00 a month for a year for her vacation. Did she have enough money for her expenses? Explain your answer.

_____

_____

_____

_____

_____

**Aloha**

# Function Tables

Completing a Function Table with up to Two Operations

**1.**

| Rule = +2.45 | |
|---|---|
| Input | Output |
| 3 | |
| 2.1 | |
| 4.16 | |
| | 5.2 |

**2.**

| Rule = −3.25 | |
|---|---|
| Input | Output |
| 5 | |
| 6.19 | |
| 7.4 | |
| | 3.5 |

**3.**

| Rule = +1 −3 | |
|---|---|
| Input | Output |
| 5 | |
| 13 | |
| 19 | |
| | 20 |

**4.**

| Rule = ×2 +1½ | |
|---|---|
| Input | Output |
| 5 | |
| 1½ | |
| 3¼ | |
| | 1½ |

**5.**

| Rule = ÷2 +1 | |
|---|---|
| Input | Output |
| 8 | |
| 12 | |
| 15 | |
| | 15.5 |

**6.**

| Rule = ×3.2 +4.9 | |
|---|---|
| Input | Output |
| 1.2 | |
| 0.8 | |
| 2 | |
| | 10.02 |

**7.**

| Rule = ÷2 +6.41 | |
|---|---|
| Input | Output |
| 4 | |
| 5 | |
| 8 | |
| | 11.91 |

**8.**

| Rule = ×⅓ +¼ | |
|---|---|
| Input | Output |
| 3 | |
| 6 | |
| 9 | |
| | 4¼ |

**9.**

| Rule = ×½ +½ | |
|---|---|
| Input | Output |
| 8 | |
| 9 | |
| 13 | |
| | 8½ |

©2005 by Evan-Moor Corp. • EMC 4550 • Math

UNIT 9  107

# What Is the Nickname for the Island of Hawai'i?

Answer each question below. Then write the corresponding letter on the line above each answer. The letters will spell out the answer to the question.

**A**   What is the percent form of $\frac{1}{2}$? _____

**B**   What is the fraction form of 30%? _____

**D**   What is the decimal form of 40%? _____

**E**   What is the fraction form of 80%? _____

**G**   What is the fraction form of 75%? _____

**H**   What is the fraction form of 0.25? _____

**I**   What is the decimal form of 43%? _____

**I**   What is the fraction form of 40%? _____

**L**   What is the decimal form of 80%? _____

**N**   What is the percent form of 0.9? _____

**S**   What is the percent form of 0.09? _____

**T**   What is the decimal form of $\frac{1}{2}$? _____

| ___ | ___ | ___ | | ___ | ___ | ___ |
|-----|-----|-----|---|-----|-----|-----|
| 0.5 | $\frac{1}{4}$ | $\frac{8}{10}$ | | $\frac{3}{10}$ | $\frac{2}{5}$ | $\frac{3}{4}$ |

| ___ | ___ | ___ | ___ | ___ | ___ |
|-----|-----|-----|-----|-----|-----|
| 0.43 | 9% | 0.8 | 50% | 90% | 0.4 |

## Remember:

Follow these steps to change a fraction to a percent:

1. Divide the numerator by the denominator.
2. Add a decimal point in the correct place.
3. Write the decimal as a fraction with 100 as the denominator.
4. Change the fraction to a percent.

**Example**

$\frac{3}{4}$

$4\overline{)3.0} = 0.75$

$0.75 = \frac{75}{100}$

$\frac{75}{100} = 75\%$

Aloha

# Scuba Gear

Jerome has been saving money so he can buy his own scuba gear. Use the information on the chart to help him determine how much money he needs.

| | |
|---|---|
| mask | $30.50 |
| fins | $51.25 |
| snorkel | $24.99 |
| boots and gloves | $36.59 |
| wet suit | $120.00 |
| regulator | $1,125.99 |

1. What is the total amount of money Jerome will need to buy everything on the list?

   _____

2. Jerome's grandparents gave him the wet suit and mask as a graduation present. Now how much will Jerome have to save?

   _____

3. If Jerome's parents agree to pay half of the remaining cost, how much will Jerome have to save?

   _____

4. Jerome has already saved $300. He plans to save half of his allowance each week until he has enough money. Jerome receives $25 a week allowance. How many weeks will it take Jerome to save the rest of the money he needs?

   _____

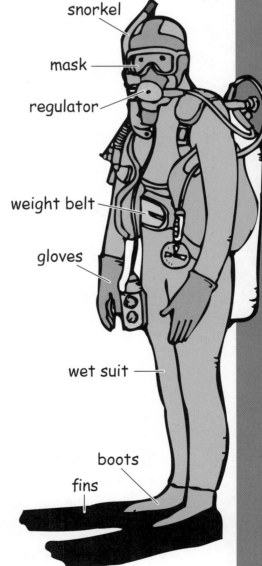

snorkel

mask

regulator

weight belt

gloves

wet suit

boots

fins

Aloha

# Shark Quiz

## How many teeth can a shark grow in its lifetime?

To find the answer, determine the Least Common Multiple (LCM) for each set of numbers below. Then write the corresponding letter on the line above the LCM. The letters will spell out the answer.

**A** What is the LCM of 1 and 5? _____

**D** What is the LCM of 2 and 3? _____

**E** What is the LCM of 3 and 9? _____

**F** What is the LCM of 1 and 11? _____

**H** What is the LCM of 16 and 2? _____

**N** What is the LCM of 17 and 1? _____

**O** What is the LCM of 13 and 1? _____

**R** What is the LCM of 18 and 3? _____

**S** What is the LCM of 14 and 2? _____

**T** What is the LCM of 3 and 5? _____

**U** What is the LCM of 1 and 7? _____

**W** What is the LCM of 2 and 5? _____

**Y** What is the LCM of 8 and 2? _____

___ ___ ___ ___ ___ ___     ___ ___ ___ ___
15  10  9   17  15  8      11  13  7   18

___ ___ ___ ___ ___ ___ ___ ___
15  16  13  7   14  5   17  6

## Remember:

The least common multiple (LCM) of two or more numbers is the smallest multiple that occurs for each number being compared. For example, the least common multiple of the following numbers is:

4 and 5—LCM is 20          2, 3, and 4—LCM is 12

Aloha

# Take a Hike

Angela's family took a long hike on Maui. Solve these problems about their hike.

1.  Angela's family went hiking and came to a bridge that has a weight limit of 500 pounds. Her father weighed 250 pounds; her aunt weighed 145 pounds; her brother weighed 48 pounds; and she weighed 65 pounds. Could they all walk on the bridge at the same time? Explain your answer.

    _____

    _____

2.  Father carried a picnic lunch for the family in his backpack. The backpack weighed 6 pounds. What did the backpack weigh after they ate lunch if each person ate the following amounts? (Remember: 16 ounces equal one pound.)

    • Father ate 28 ounces of food.
    • Angela's aunt ate 20 ounces of food.
    • Angela's brother ate 10 ounces of food.
    • Angela ate 14 ounces of food.

    _____

3.  Angela started out with a full canteen of water. During the first hour, she drank $\frac{1}{4}$ of the water. During the next hour, she drank $\frac{1}{2}$ of what was left. How full was her canteen at the end of the hike?

    _____

4.  The family kept a log of the changes in elevation each half hour. They started the hike at an elevation of 6,080 feet. The changes in elevation for the hike were +45, +200, −80, +35, −20, and +110. What was the elevation at the end of their hike?

    _____

# Hiking Trails

**Skills:**

Using an
Organized List
to Determine
All Possible
Combinations

The following map represents different trails from the park entrance to the top of the dormant volcano. Make an ordered list to show four of the eight possible trails from the entrance to Volcano Peak, without going on any trail more than once during a single route.

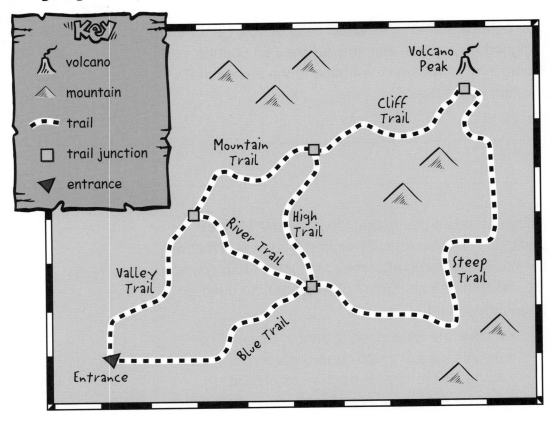

_____

_____

_____

_____

_____

_____

_____

_____

Aloha

# What Did They Do?

Complete this logic puzzle to determine what each family did during its trip to the Hawaiian Islands.

|  | scuba diving | surfing | hiking | kayaking | fishing | bicycling |
|---|---|---|---|---|---|---|
| Adams |  |  |  |  |  |  |
| Chen |  |  |  |  |  |  |
| Hernandez |  |  |  |  |  |  |
| Jordan |  |  |  |  |  |  |
| Probst |  |  |  |  |  |  |
| Rice |  |  |  |  |  |  |

## Clues

★ Each family participated in a different activity.

★ The Rice family went bicycling.

★ The Hernandez family did not go hiking.

★ The Jordan family went scuba diving.

★ The Chen family and the family who went hiking have both been to Hawai'i before.

★ The Adams family went for a longer time than the Hernandez family, but not as long as the family that went fishing.

★ The Probst family went surfing.

### Remember:

See page 24 if you need a reminder on how to do a logic puzzle.

Aloha

Note: Use this assessment after your child has completed through page 113.

Fill in the circle next to the correct answer.

1. +9 + ⁻2 = _____
   Ⓐ +11   Ⓒ +7
   Ⓑ ⁻11   Ⓓ ⁻12

2. ⁻5 + ⁻12 = _____
   Ⓐ +17   Ⓒ ⁻7
   Ⓑ +7    Ⓓ ⁻17

3. What is the decimal form of $\frac{1}{2}$?
   Ⓐ 0.25   Ⓒ 0.12
   Ⓑ 0.5    Ⓓ 0.1

4. What is the fraction form of 25%?
   Ⓐ $\frac{1}{2}$   Ⓒ $\frac{5}{7}$
   Ⓑ $\frac{2}{3}$   Ⓓ $\frac{1}{4}$

5. What is the percent form of $\frac{9}{10}$?
   Ⓐ 9%    Ⓒ 10%
   Ⓑ 90%   Ⓓ 91%

6. What does LCM stand for?
   Ⓐ Lowest Computed Multiple
   Ⓑ Least Computed Measurement
   Ⓒ Least Common Multiple
   Ⓓ Longitudinal Cartesian Measurement

7. What is the LCM of 9 and 12?
   Ⓐ 72   Ⓒ 1
   Ⓑ 3    Ⓓ 36

Use this number line for numbers 8 and 9.

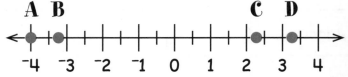

8. Which point is located at $2\frac{1}{4}$?
   Ⓐ point A   Ⓒ point C
   Ⓑ point B   Ⓓ point D

9. Which point is located at $^-3\frac{1}{3}$?
   Ⓐ point A   Ⓒ point C
   Ⓑ point B   Ⓓ point D

Use this function table for numbers 10 through 12.

| Rule = ÷2 +4 | |
| --- | --- |
| Input | Output |
| 4 | |
| 7 | |
| | 16 |

10. What is the output if the input is 4?
    Ⓐ 6   Ⓒ 6.5
    Ⓑ 7   Ⓓ 7.5

11. What is the output if the input is 7?
    Ⓐ 6   Ⓒ 6.5
    Ⓑ 7   Ⓓ 7.5

12. What is the input if the output is 16?
    Ⓐ 24   Ⓒ 16
    Ⓑ 20   Ⓓ 12

**114**   **ASSESSMENT 9**   Math · EMC 4550 · ©2005 by Evan-Moor Corp.

# Space Quiz

## What are the planets Jupiter, Saturn, Uranus, and Neptune called?

To find the answer to this space question, solve each problem below.
Write the corresponding letter on the line above the correct answer.
The letters will spell out the answer.

A   $4^3$ = _____

A   $8^2$ = _____

G   $6^2$ = _____

G   $3^3$ = _____

I   $5^3$ = _____

N   $5^2$ = _____

S   $9^2$ = _____

S   $7^2$ = _____

T   $2^5$ = _____

_____   _____   _____
36      64      81

_____   _____   _____   _____   _____   _____
27      125     64      25      32      49

Outer Space

# Mystery Word

**Skills:**

Locating Points on a Number Line

Look at each value given below. Locate the value on the number line and write the corresponding letter above the number line. The letters will spell out the mystery word when read from left to right.

| | | | | | |
|---|---|---|---|---|---|
| 4 | **A** | −14 | **C** | −3 | **E** |
| 9 | **I** | 2 | **L** | 0 | **L** |
| 13 | **N** | −10 | **N** | 10 | **O** |
| −12 | **O** | −7 | **S** | 15 | **S** |
| 6 | **T** | −5 | **T** | | |

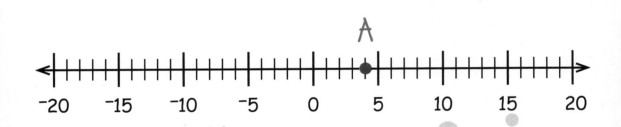

Fill in the circle in front of the meaning of the mystery word.

◯ the name for groups of planets orbiting a sun

◯ a body in space with a solid mass and a tail of gas and dust

◯ various groups of stars that have been given names

**Outer Space**

Math • EMC 4550 • ©2005 by Evan-Moor Corp.

# Space Map

Pictured here is a space map. Use the map to answer the questions below.

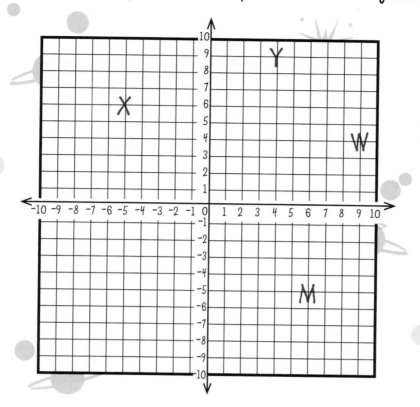

**1.** The *X* marks a planet. What is the ordered pair for that location? _____

**2.** A comet is located at (9, 4) and a star is located at (4, 9). Which letter marks each location?

   comet _____          star _____

**3.** The *M* marks a moon. What is the ordered pair for that location? _____

**4.** A spaceship is ready to take off from the intersection at (⁻2, ⁻4). It is heading to a black hole at the intersection of (6, ⁻8). Plot each location on the space map. Label the spaceship *S* and the black hole *B*.

## Remember:

- Start at the 0.
- Move across (horizontally) first, and then up or down (vertically).
- (4, 3) means move to the right 4 blocks and then move up 3 blocks.
- (⁻6, ⁻3) means move to the left 6 blocks, and then move down 3 blocks.

Outer Space

# Blast Off!

Plot the ordered pairs of numbers in the order in which they are listed. Connect them with straight lines. Start each new set of points with a new line.

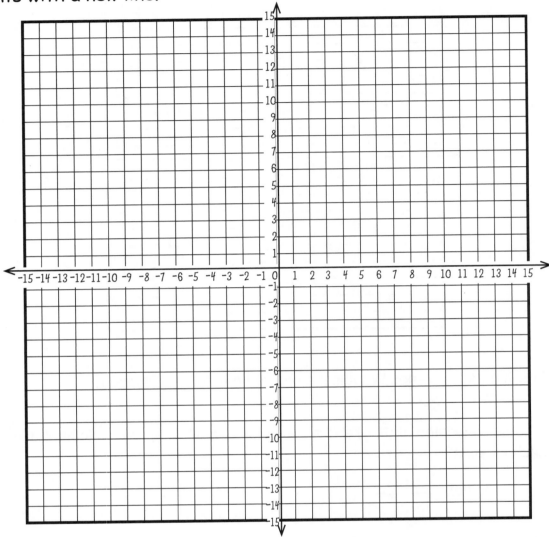

▶ (−5, −9) (−8, −9) (−8, −4) (−5, 1) (−5, 10) (−1, 14) (0, 14) (4, 10) (4, 1) (7, −4) (7, −9) (4, −9) line ends

▶ (−5, 1) (−5, −10) (4, −10) (4, 1) line ends

▶ (−4, −10) (−4, −14) line ends

▶ (−3, −10) (−3, −14) line ends

▶ (−2, −10) (−2, −14) line ends

▶ (1, −10) (1, −14) line ends

▶ (2, −10) (2, −14) line ends

▶ (3, −10) (3, −14) line ends

▶ (1, 10) (1, 7) (3, 7) (3, 10) line ends

▶ (1, 1) (3, 1) (3, 3) (1, 3) (1, 5) (3, 5) line ends

▶ (1, −5) (1, −3) (2, −1) (3, −3) (3, −5) line ends

▶ (1, −3) (3, −3) line ends

# Tongue Twister

Complete each division problem below. Write the corresponding letter on the line above the correct answer. The letters will spell out a tongue twister. Try to say it fast five times. Good luck!

**A**   24.0 ÷ 40.0 = _____

**A**   7.2 ÷ 2.4 = _____

**C**   20.0 ÷ 50.0 = _____

**C**   0.1 ÷ 0.5 = _____

**E**   28.8 ÷ 6.0 = _____

**E**   0.96 ÷ 0.3 = _____

**P**   2.4 ÷ 2.0 = _____

**R**   1.26 ÷ 0.6 = _____

**S**   0.5 ÷ 0.2 = _____

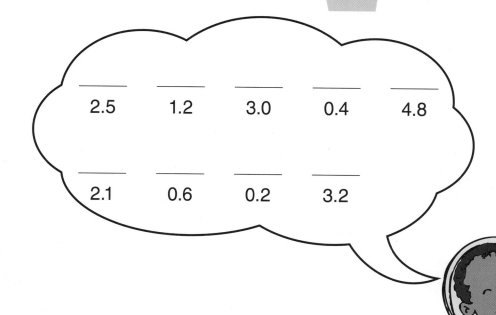

_____   _____   _____   _____   _____
2.5      1.2      3.0      0.4      4.8

_____   _____   _____   _____
2.1      0.6      0.2      3.2

**Outer Space**

# Vast Distances of Space

**Skills:**

Determining
Place Value
and Rounding
Numbers to
Millions

Distances in outer space are very large. Rounding the numbers can make them easier to read. Round each of these "vast" numbers to the requested place value.

1. 280 to the nearest hundred _____

2. 49,305 to the nearest thousand _____

3. 27,539 to the nearest ten _____

4. 184,390 to the nearest ten thousand _____

5. 286,952 to the nearest hundred thousand _____

6. 1,682,842 to the nearest hundred thousand _____

7. 5,930,206 to the nearest million _____

8. 7,502,401 to the nearest hundred thousand _____

9. 3,202,294 to the nearest million _____

10. 15,392,487 to the nearest million _____

## Remember:

Round down from numbers under 5. (Use the same rule for numbers under 50, 500, 5,000, etc.) Round up from numbers 5 or greater. (Use the same rule for numbers 50 and above; 500 and above; 5,000 and above; etc.)

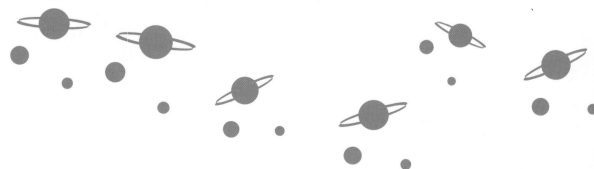

Outer Space

# Make It Metric

Change each planet's diameter from a customary to a metric amount.

**Skills:**
Converting Customary Measure to Metric Measure

## Diameters of Planets

| | Planet | Miles | Kilometers |
|---|---|---|---|
| 1. | Mercury | 3,031 | |
| 2. | Venus | 7,521 | |
| 3. | Earth | 7,926 | |
| 4. | Mars | 4,222 | |
| 5. | Jupiter | 88,729 | |
| 6. | Saturn | 74,600 | |
| 7. | Uranus | 32,600 | |
| 8. | Neptune | 30,200 | |

### Remember:

To change a distance from miles to kilometers, multiply by 1.61.

100 miles × 1.61 = 161 kilometers

©2005 by Evan-Moor Corp. • EMC 4550 • Math

**UNIT 10**

Outer Space

# Compute My Data

Skills:

Analyzing
Data Utilizing
Range, Mean,
Median, and
Mode

Complete the following chart.

| | Set of Data | Range | Mean | Median | Mode |
|---|---|---|---|---|---|
| **1.** | 15, 23, 23, 24, 26 | | | | |
| **2.** | 1, 2, 4, 4, 4, 5, 8, 9 | | | | |
| **3.** | 6, 6, 6, 6, 6, 6, 6, | | | | |
| **4.** | 21, 23, 25, 28, 32, 39 | | | | |
| **5.** | 40, 45, 50, 55, 60, 65, 70 | | | | |

### Remember:

Check page 54 if you need help with this page.

**Outer Space**

122    **UNIT 10**

# Race Across Space

Subtract the numbers to help the astronaut reach the distant planet.

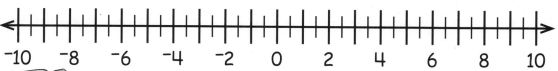

$^-5 - {}^+2 = $ _____

$^-10 - {}^-6 = $ _____

$^-2 - {}^-3 = $ _____

$^-7 - {}^+3 = $ _____

$^-2 - {}^+4 = $ _____

$^+2 - {}^-7 = $ _____

$^-8 - {}^-7 = $ _____

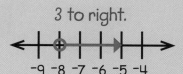

## Remember:

- When you subtract a negative number, you move to the right on a number line.

$^-8 - {}^-3 = \mathbf{?}$

Start at $^-8$ on the number line and move 3 to the right.

The answer is $^-5$.

3 to right.

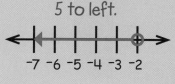

- When you subtract a positive number, you move to the left on the number line.

$^-2 - {}^+5 = \mathbf{?}$

Start at $^-2$ on the number line and move 5 to the left.

The answer is $^-7$.

5 to left.

**Outer Space**

# What's a Cat's Favorite Part of Outer Space?

**Skills:**

Identifying
Congruent
Shapes

Look at each figure in the box. Find the shape at the bottom of the page that is congruent (same shape and size) to the white region. Write the corresponding letter on the line above the congruent shape. The letters will spell out the solution to the riddle.

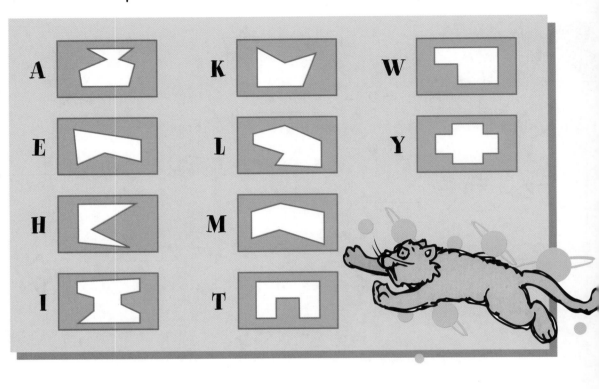

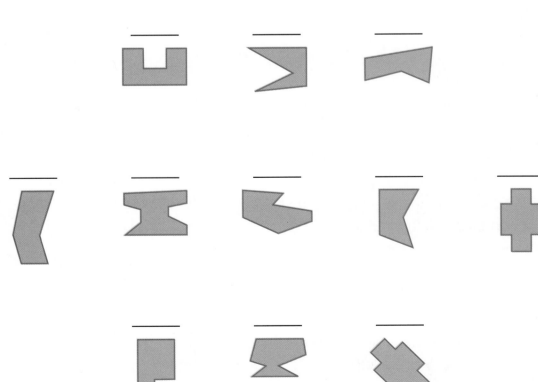

Outer Space

# Transform Me

Sketch what each figure will be after the given transformations.

**1.** Translate to the right.

**2.** Rotate to the left 90 degrees.

**3.** Reflect across the dashed line.

**4.** Translate to the right.

**5.** Reflect across the dashed line.

**Outer Space**

---

**Remember:**

If you need help with this task, read page 49.

# It's in the Bag

**Skills:**

Computing
Theoretical
Probabilities
for Simple
Chance Events

Jason and Maria were playing the probability game with toy spaceships. Jake put 4 red spaceships and 8 blue spaceships in a bag. What is the probability of Maria randomly selecting a spaceship that is...?

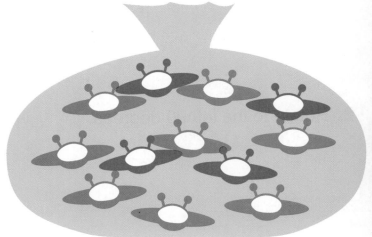

**1.** red  $\dfrac{4}{12} = \dfrac{1}{3}$

**2.** blue  _____

**3.** gold  _____

Next, they took turns spinning this spinner, what is the probability of getting...?

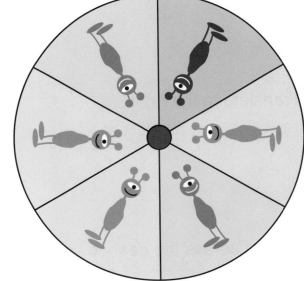

**4.** green  _____

**5.** purple  _____

**6.** orange  _____

> ### Remember:
>
> **Probability** tells the likelihood something will happen. It is usually written as a fraction.
>
> 1 red spaceship, 1 blue spaceship in a bag
>
> The probability is one in two chances ($\frac{1}{2}$) that you will draw either color spaceship from the bag.

Outer Space

**TEST YOUR SKILLS**

Fill in the circle next to the correct answer.

**1.** $4^3 =$ _____

Ⓐ 16          Ⓒ 72

Ⓑ 64          Ⓓ 20

**2.** $8^2 =$ _____

Ⓐ 10          Ⓒ 16

Ⓑ 512         Ⓓ 64

**3.** $3^4 =$ _____

Ⓐ 9           Ⓒ 27

Ⓑ 18          Ⓓ 81

**4.** 0.096 ÷ 1.2 = _____

Ⓐ 80.0        Ⓒ 0.8

Ⓑ 8.0         Ⓓ 0.08

**5.** 4.68 ÷ 5.2 = _____

Ⓐ 9.0         Ⓒ 0.09

Ⓑ 0.9         Ⓓ 0.0009

**6.** Round 345 to the nearest hundred.

Ⓐ 400         Ⓒ 350

Ⓑ 300         Ⓓ 455

**7.** Round 56,205 to the nearest thousand.

Ⓐ 57,000      Ⓒ 56,200

Ⓑ 56,000      Ⓓ 57,200

**8.** Round 175,832 to the nearest ten thousand.

Ⓐ 100,000     Ⓒ 180,000

Ⓑ 170,000     Ⓓ 176,000

For numbers 9 through 12, use this graph.

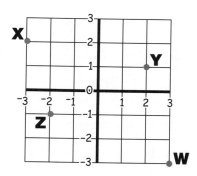

**9.** What is the ordered pair for point **W**?

Ⓐ (3, 3)      Ⓒ (−3, 3)

Ⓑ (3, −3)     Ⓓ (−3, −3)

**10.** What is the ordered pair for point **X**?

Ⓐ (3, 2)      Ⓒ (−3, 2)

Ⓑ (3, −2)     Ⓓ (−3, −2)

**11.** What is the ordered pair for point **Y**?

Ⓐ (2, 1)      Ⓒ (−2, 1)

Ⓑ (2, −1)     Ⓓ (−2, −1)

**12.** What is the ordered pair for point **Z**?

Ⓐ (2, 1)      Ⓒ (−2, 1)

Ⓑ (2, −1)     Ⓓ (−2, −1)

## Fill in the circle next to the correct answer.

**Use this number line for numbers 1 through 4.**

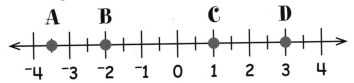

**1.** Which point is located at −2?

Ⓐ point **A**   Ⓒ point **C**

Ⓑ point **B**   Ⓓ point **D**

**2.** Which point is located at 3?

Ⓐ point **A**   Ⓒ point **C**

Ⓑ point **B**   Ⓓ point **D**

**3.** Which point is located at 1?

Ⓐ point **A**   Ⓒ point **C**

Ⓑ point **B**   Ⓓ point **D**

**4.** Which point is located at −3.5?

Ⓐ point **A**   Ⓒ point **C**

Ⓑ point **B**   Ⓓ point **D**

**5.** Draw a number line and number it from −3 to +3, with 0 right in the middle. Write an **S** on the value of −1 and a **W** on the value of 2.

**For numbers 6 and 7, use this bag of marbles.**

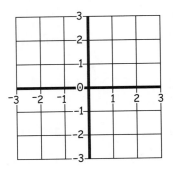

**6.** What is the probability of drawing a white marble at random from the bag?

Ⓐ $\frac{1}{2}$   Ⓑ $\frac{1}{3}$   Ⓒ $\frac{2}{11}$   Ⓓ $\frac{2}{9}$

**7.** What is the probability of drawing a black marble at random from the bag?

Ⓐ $\frac{1}{2}$   Ⓑ $\frac{9}{11}$   Ⓒ $\frac{3}{6}$   Ⓓ $\frac{3}{4}$

**For numbers 8 through 11, use the following data:**

25, 27, 28, 29, 29, 30, 32, 35, 35

**8.** What is the mean of the data set?

Ⓐ 19   Ⓑ 30   Ⓒ 31   Ⓓ 32

**9.** What is the range of the data set?

Ⓐ 25   Ⓑ 10   Ⓒ 15   Ⓓ 35

**10.** What is the mode of the data set?

Ⓐ 29          Ⓒ both 29 and 35

Ⓑ 35          Ⓓ there is no mode

**11.** What is the median of the data set?

Ⓐ 29   Ⓑ 30   Ⓒ 32   Ⓓ 35

**12.** Plot point A at (−2, 1) and point B at (0, −2) on this graph.

# Tracking Form

| Topic | Color in each page you complete. | | | | | | |
|---|---|---|---|---|---|---|---|
| | 3 | 4 | 5 | 6 | 7 | 8 | 9 |
| Deep Blue Sea | 10 | 11 | 12 | 13 | 14 | | |
| Collections | 15 | 16 | 17 | 18 | 19 | 20 | 21 |
| | 22 | 23 | 24 | 25 | 26 | 27 | |
| Pizza Party | 28 | 29 | 30 | 31 | 32 | 33 | 34 |
| | 35 | 36 | 37 | 38 | 39 | | |
| Yard Sale | 40 | 41 | 42 | 43 | 44 | 45 | 46 |
| | 47 | 48 | 49 | 50 | 51 | 52 | |
| Play Ball | 53 | 54 | 55 | 56 | 57 | 58 | 59 |
| | 60 | 61 | 62 | 63 | 64 | | |
| Lines, Angles, Shapes | 65 | 66 | 67 | 68 | 69 | 70 | 71 |
| | 72 | 73 | 74 | 75 | 76 | 77 | |
| At the Mall | 78 | 79 | 80 | 81 | 82 | 83 | 84 |
| | 85 | 86 | 87 | 88 | 89 | | |
| Math Recipes | 90 | 91 | 92 | 93 | 94 | 95 | 96 |
| | 97 | 98 | 99 | 100 | 101 | 102 | |
| Aloha | 103 | 104 | 105 | 106 | 107 | 108 | 109 |
| | 110 | 111 | 112 | 113 | 114 | | |
| Outer Space | 115 | 116 | 117 | 118 | 119 | 120 | 121 |
| | 122 | 123 | 124 | 125 | 126 | 127 | 128 |

ed numbers **indicate Test Your Skills pages.**

# Answer Key

## Page 3

| | | |
|---|---|---|
| **1.** 15,201 | **7.** 4,571 | **13.** 50 |
| **2.** 15,028 | **8.** 5,367 | **14.** 215 |
| **3.** 6,710 | **9.** 60,408 | **15.** 52 |
| **4.** 12,102 | **10.** 8,208 | **16.** 420 |
| **5.** 2,916 | **11.** 102,088 | |
| **6.** 3,049 | **12.** 473,623 | |

Answers in order from smallest to largest:
50; 52; 215; 420;
2,916; 3,049; 4,571; 5,367;
6,710; 8,208; 12,102; 15,028;
15,201; 60,408; 102,088; 473,623

## Page 4

| | | | |
|---|---|---|---|
| **A** $24 \times 73 =$ | _1,752_ | **N** $329 \times 89 =$ | _29,281_ |
| **B** $81 \times 94 =$ | _7,614_ | **O** $104 \times 53 =$ | _5,512_ |
| **C** $32 \times 95 =$ | _3,040_ | **S** $210 \times 42 =$ | _8,820_ |
| **E** $38 \times 72 =$ | _2,736_ | **T** $2,952 \times 15 =$ | _44,280_ |
| **H** $40 \times 102 =$ | _4,080_ | **U** $4,201 \times 20 =$ | _84,020_ |
| **I** $804 \times 18 =$ | _14,472_ | **V** $285 \times 21 =$ | _5,985_ |
| **L** $412 \times 21 =$ | _8,652_ | **Y** $235 \times 28 =$ | _6,580_ |

B / E / C / A / U / S / E
7,614 / 2,736 / 3,040 / 1,752 / 84,020 / 8,820 / 2,736

T / H / E / Y
44,280 / 4,080 / 2,736 / 6,580

L / I / V / E / I / N
8,652 / 14,472 / 5,985 / 2,736 / 14,472 / 29,281

S / C / H / O / O / L / S
8,820 / 3,040 / 4,080 / 5,512 / 5,512 / 8,652 / 8,820

## Page 5

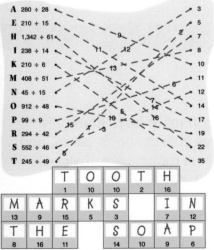

| A | $280 \div 28$ | | 3 |
| E | $210 \div 15$ | | 5 |
| H | $1,342 \div 61$ | | 7 |
| I | $238 \div 14$ | | 8 |
| K | $210 \div 6$ | | 10 |
| M | $408 \div 51$ | | 11 |
| N | $45 \div 15$ | | 12 |
| O | $912 \div 48$ | | 14 |
| P | $99 \div 9$ | | 17 |
| R | $294 \div 42$ | | 19 |
| S | $552 \div 46$ | | 22 |
| T | $245 \div 49$ | | 35 |

| T | O | O | T | H | |
|---|---|---|---|---|---|
| 1 | 10 | 10 | 2 | 16 | |

| M | A | R | K | S | | I | N |
|---|---|---|---|---|---|---|---|
| 13 | 9 | 15 | 5 | 3 | | 7 | 12 |

| T | H | E | | S | O | A | P |
|---|---|---|---|---|---|---|---|
| 8 | 16 | 11 | | 14 | 10 | 9 | 6 |

## Page 6

SIX CRISP SHRIMP

## Page 7

**1.** 9,875
**2.** 27,409
**3.** 635,956
**4.** 8,600,227
**5.** four thousand, six hundred eighty-nine
**6.** twenty-seven thousand, two hundred five
**7.** six hundred forty-three thousand, eight hundred seventeen
**8.** one million, three hundred nine thousand, seven hundred sixty-two
**9.** 200 + 600 + 80 + 3
**10.** 10,000 + 6,000 + 500 + 20
**11.** 500,000 + 80,000 + 7,000 + 400
**12.** 4,000,000 + 300,000 + 5,000 + 800 + 90 + 1

## Page 8

**1.** Rule = +27

| Input | Output |
|---|---|
| 1 | 28 |
| 11 | 38 |
| 16 | 43 |
| 23 | 50 |

**2.** Rule = −15

| Input | Output |
|---|---|
| 25 | 10 |
| 19 | 4 |
| 15 | 0 |
| 13 | −2 |

**3.** Rule = +4 −3

| Input | Output |
|---|---|
| 4 | 5 |
| 15 | 16 |
| 23 | 24 |
| 34 | 35 |

**4.** Rule = ×2 +3

| Input | Output |
|---|---|
| 2 | 7 |
| 4 | 11 |
| 9 | 21 |
| 15 | 33 |

**5.** Rule = ÷2 +1

| Input | Output |
|---|---|
| 4 | 3 |
| 16 | 9 |
| 24 | 13 |
| 38 | 20 |

**6.** Rule = ×3 −5

| Input | Output |
|---|---|
| 19 | 52 |
| 15 | 40 |
| 8 | 19 |
| 1 | −2 |

**7.** Rule = ×3 −12

| Input | Output |
|---|---|
| 12 | 24 |
| 8 | 12 |
| 5 | 3 |
| 3 | −3 |

**8.** Rule = ÷3 −2

| Input | Output |
|---|---|
| 12 | 2 |
| 15 | 3 |
| 21 | 5 |
| 39 | 11 |

**9.** Rule = ×5 +1

| Input | Output |
|---|---|
| 3 | 16 |
| 4 | 21 |
| 8 | 41 |
| 10 | 51 |

## Page 9

A  $15 + 6 \times 2 =$  __27__
C  $20 + 10 \div 5 =$  __22__
R  $9 + 2 \times 5 =$  __19__
O  $14 + 1 \times 3 =$  __17__

D  $18 \times 6 \div 2 =$  __54__
E  $6 \times (3 + 1) =$  __24__
S  $16 - 4 \div 4 =$  __15__
S  $7 + 4 \times 2 =$  __15__
A  $33 - 3 \times 2 =$  __27__
R  $5 \times 2 + 9 =$  __19__
R  $26 - (9 - 2) =$  __19__
A  $8 \times 4 - 5 =$  __27__
B  $15 \times (3 - 3) =$  __0__
M  $19 - (10 - 5) =$  __14__
E  $26 - 6 \div 3 =$  __24__

N  $12 \div 3 + 1 =$  __5__
A  $30 - 9 \div 3 =$  __27__

## Page 10

1. Note to Timothy should disagree. The answer to a) is 19, and the answer to b) is 15.
2. Note to Francine should agree. The answer to the problem would be 14 whether or not the parentheses are used.
3. Note to Drew should list the following steps: first multiply $4 \times 3$ to get 12; then add the $5 + 12$ inside the parentheses to get 17; then, going from left to right, subtract $90 - 17$ to get 73; then add 73 to 30 to get the correct answer 103.

## Page 11

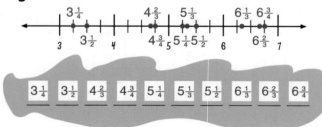

## Page 12

| Total Cost | Number of People in the Group | Each Person in the Group Paid |
|---|---|---|
| $18.75 | five | $ 3.75 |
| $43.50 | three | $ 14.50 |
| $31.40 | four | $ 7.85 |
| $ 146.40 | twenty | $7.32 |
| $ 52.40 | eight | $6.55 |
| $93.50 | eleven | $ 8.50 |
| $ 1,350 | fifteen | $90.00 |
| $ 85.50 | six | $14.25 |
| $144.00 | twelve | $ 12.00 |

## Page 13

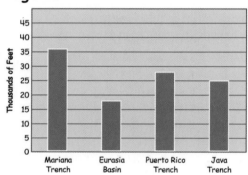

How much deeper is the deepest part of the Pacific Ocean than the deepest part of the Indian Ocean?

__11,000 feet__

## Page 14

1. C
2. C
3. A
4. D
5. C
6. B
7. D
8. C
9. C
10. C
11. D
12. A

Unit 2

## Page 15

1. 640 students
2. More boys; 60 more boys than girls
3. No; 100 boys collect sports cards, and 60 boys collect model cars. Twice 60 would be 120, not 100.

## Page 15 (continued)

4. No; 50 girls collect stamps, and 90 girls collect charms. Half as many girls would be 45, not 50.

## Page 16

1. 1,244 cards
2. $17.10
3. Amy has 100 cards.
4. 126 feet (1,512 inches)

## Page 17

1. $10.00
2. About $132.00

## Page 18

1. $44.94
2. 4:15 P.M.
3. cylinder; a cylinder has a two bases shaped like circles; a cone has 1 base shaped like a circle, and the curved side meets at a point.
4. 23 sets
5. 60 CDs

## Page 19

1. 6 minutes
2. 10.8 minutes or 10 minutes 48 seconds
3. 12 minutes longer

## Page 20

1. 12 model cars
2. $3.75
3. $195.00
4. July
5. $42.50

## Page 21

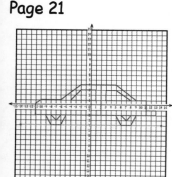

## Page 22

1. Rick has 175 stamps and Myra has 325 stamps.
2. $6.30
3. 72¢
4. 90 stamps

## Page 23

1. $8 \times 6 \times 3 = 144$ cubic inches
2. $12 \times 6 \times 6 = 432$ cubic inches
3. $8 \times 4 \times 3 = 96$ cubic inches
4. $18 \times 12 \times 4 = 864$ cubic inches

## Page 24

|  | Black | Blue | Green | Red | 315 | 720 | 1,205 | 2,403 |
|---|---|---|---|---|---|---|---|---|
| Erik | X | X | X | YES | YES | X | X | X |
| Jerry | X | YES | X | X | X | X | X | YES |
| Carol | X | X | YES | X | X | X | YES | X |
| Sandy | YES | X | X | X | X | YES | X | X |

## Page 25

1. 25
2. 6
3. 12
4. 35
5. 24
6. 36
7. 7
8. 16
9. 42
10. 5
11. 63
12. 27
13. 5
14. 7
15. 24
16. 63

## Page 26

1. $27
2. $38
3. $6
4. $18

## Page 27

1. B
2. D
3. A
4. C
5. A
6. A
7. D
8. B
9. A
10. C
11. D

12.

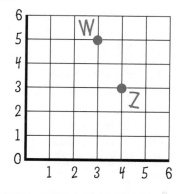

Unit 3

## Page 28

1. $\frac{2}{15}$
2. $\frac{3}{28}$
3. $\frac{3}{16}$
4. $\frac{9}{28}$
5. $\frac{5}{27}$
6. $5\frac{1}{4}$
7. $2\frac{1}{7}$
8. $10\frac{2}{7}$
9. $3\frac{17}{20}$
10. $15\frac{3}{4}$

## Page 29

$\underline{S}$   $\frac{3}{4} \div \frac{1}{2} = 1\frac{1}{2}$     $\underline{P}$   $\frac{2}{4} \div \frac{2}{3} = \frac{3}{4}$

$\underline{P}$   $\frac{1}{2} \div \frac{2}{3} = \frac{3}{4}$     $\underline{I}$   $\frac{8}{10} \div \frac{3}{5} = 1\frac{1}{3}$

$\underline{I}$   $\frac{4}{5} \div \frac{3}{5} = 1\frac{1}{3}$     $\underline{Z}$   $\frac{3}{4} \div \frac{1}{3} = 2\frac{1}{4}$

$\underline{C}$   $\frac{2}{3} \div \frac{5}{6} = \frac{4}{5}$     $\underline{Z}$   $\frac{6}{8} \div \frac{1}{3} = 2\frac{1}{4}$

$\underline{Y}$   $\frac{4}{7} \div \frac{1}{2} = 1\frac{1}{7}$     $\underline{A}$   $\frac{4}{5} \div \frac{2}{5} = 2$

## Page 30

1. $\frac{1}{2} \div 2 = \frac{1}{2} \times \frac{1}{2} = \frac{1}{4}$

2. $\frac{3}{4} \div \frac{6}{1} = \frac{3}{4} \times \frac{1}{6} = \frac{3}{24} = \frac{1}{8}$

3. $2 \div \frac{1}{3} = \frac{2}{1} \times \frac{3}{1} = \frac{6}{1} = 6$

4. $5\frac{1}{3} \div 1\frac{1}{3} = \frac{16}{3} \div \frac{4}{3} =$ $\frac{16}{3} \times \frac{3}{4} = \frac{48}{12} = 4$

## Page 31

1. $54.25     3. $9.40

2. 3 pieces     4. $44.85

## Page 32

$\underline{I}$   $0.7 \times 0.4 = \underline{0.28}$     $\underline{M}$   $5.1 \times 2.6 = \underline{13.26}$

$\underline{N}$   $0.2 \times 0.3 = \underline{0.06}$     $\underline{O}$   $0.36 \times 2 = \underline{0.72}$

$\underline{Y}$   $0.9 \times 0.4 = \underline{0.36}$     $\underline{U}$   $1.29 \times 0.3 = \underline{0.387}$

$\underline{O}$   $1.2 \times 0.6 = \underline{0.72}$     $\underline{T}$   $1.8 \times 6.4 = \underline{11.52}$

$\underline{U}$   $4.3 \times 0.09 = \underline{0.387}$     $\underline{H}$   $0.17 \times 2.1 = \underline{0.357}$

$\underline{R}$   $1.2 \times 1.3 = \underline{1.56}$

## Page 33

1. 3.2    3. 5.2    5. 2.2    7. 0.11

2. 4.6    4. 6.54    6. 0.23    8. 200

## Page 34

| 1. $2 \overline{)18}$ $3 \overline{)9}$ $3$ $2 \times 3 \times 3$ | 2. $2 \overline{)20}$ $2 \overline{)10}$ $5$ $2 \times 2 \times 5$ | 3. $2 \overline{)24}$ $2 \overline{)12}$ $2 \overline{)6}$ $3$ $2 \times 2 \times 2 \times 3$ |
|---|---|---|
| 4. $3 \overline{)15}$ $5$ $3 \times 5$ | 5. $2 \overline{)30}$ $3 \overline{)15}$ $5$ $2 \times 3 \times 5$ | 6. $2 \overline{)22}$ $11$ $2 \times 11$ |

## Page 35

1. 2    3. 5    5. 2    7. 2

2. 3    4. 4    6. 5    8. 12

## Page 36

1. $\frac{1}{3}$    4. $\frac{3}{4}$    7. $\frac{4}{5}$    10. $\frac{6}{7}$

2. $\frac{1}{3}$    5. $\frac{4}{7}$    8. $\frac{5}{6}$

3. $\frac{1}{2}$    6. $\frac{1}{3}$    9. $\frac{1}{3}$

## Page 37

| 3.8 | 4.2 | 4.7 | 4.8 | 4.9 | 5.2 | 5.5 | 5.8 | 6.2 | 6.5 |

## Page 38

1. $3.14 \times 3 = 9.42$ in.

2. $3.14 \times 8 = 25.12$ in.

3. $3.14 \times 4 = 12.56$ in.

4. $3.14 \times 12 = 37.68$ in.

5. $3.14 \times 10 = 31.4$ in.

## Page 39

1. A    4. B    7. D    10. B

2. B    5. B    8. C    11. C

3. C    6. B    9. D    12. B

## Page 40

1. $9\frac{1}{2}$ hours
2. $5.41
3. 1 five-dollar bill, 1 quarter, 1 dime, 1 nickel, and 1 penny
4. $10.75

## Page 41

1. Nancy $3.45; John $5.75; Susan $5.00; Scott $5.05; Judy $3.10
2. $4.47

## Page 42

1. $14.87
2. 48 cups
3. $20.25
4. $5.38
5. Yes. Two tickets cost $5.00 and they made $5.38.

## Page 43

1. 3 hours and 38 minutes
2. 3 hours and 38 minutes
3. 4 hours and 28 minutes
4. 5 hours and 18 minutes
5. 3 hours
6. 3 hours and 38 minutes
7. 3 hours and 18 minutes
8. 8 hours
9. 5 hours

## Page 44

## Page 45

Perimeter is 80 feet.
Area is 276 square feet.

## Page 46

1. Felton family
2. $200
3. $2,000
4. $200

## Page 47

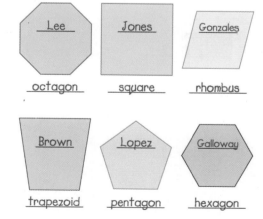

## Page 48

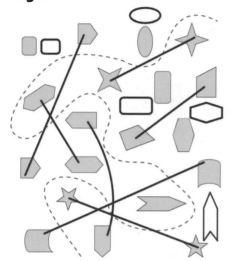

## Page 49

1. turned
2. flipped or turned
3. slid
4. flipped or turned
5. flipped or turned
6. turned
7. flipped or turned
8. slid

## Page 50

FIVE FAT GOLDFISH

## Page 51

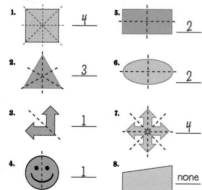

## Page 52

| | | |
|---|---|---|
| 1. C | 4. C | 7. B |
| 2. D | 5. C | 8. A |
| 3. B | 6. B | 9. B |

## Page 52 (continued)

10. Answers will vary, but child's name should appear to be slid to the right.

11. D          12. D

## Page 53

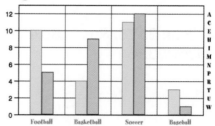

2. Each line below has a sport and a gender listed under it. This corresponds to one of the bars you drew on the graph. Go to the top of each bar and look horizontally to the right and you will see a letter. Write this letter on the corresponding line, and it will spell out the answer to the riddle.

C   A   R   P   E   T

## Page 54

| | | |
|---|---|---|
| 1. 18 | 5. 57 | 9. 36 |
| 2. 19 | 6. 34.5 | 10. 8 |
| 3. 40 | 7. 11 | 11. 61 |
| 4. 8 | 8. 55 | 12. There is no mode. |

## Page 55

| | | |
|---|---|---|
| 1. 12 feet | 5. 7 yards | 9. 27 yards |
| 2. 76 feet | 6. 11 yards | 10. 8 yards |
| 3. 2 feet | 7. 180 inches | |
| 4. 210 inches | 8. 150 feet | |

## Page 56

A   40   centimeters = 400 millimeters

T   1,000 centimeters = 10   meters

O   2   meters = 200 centimeters

U   50   meters = 5,000 centimeters

C   100   centimeters = 1,000 millimeters

H   30 millimeters = 3   centimeters

D   1   meter = 1,000 millimeters

O   2   kilometers = 2,000 meters

W   6,000 meters = 6   kilometers

N   4   kilometers = 4,000 meters

## Page 57

| | | |
|---|---|---|
| **T** | $\frac{2}{3} + \frac{3}{4} =$ | $1\frac{5}{12}$ |
| **O** | $\frac{1}{2} \times \frac{1}{2} =$ | $\frac{1}{4}$ |
| **S** | $8\frac{1}{3} - 3\frac{1}{2} =$ | $4\frac{5}{6}$ |
| **B** | $\frac{2}{3} \div \frac{1}{3} =$ | $2$ |
| **M** | $2\frac{1}{4} + 3\frac{1}{2} =$ | $5\frac{3}{4}$ |
| **E** | $\frac{6}{8} \div \frac{2}{5} =$ | $1\frac{4}{5}$ |
| **A** | $7\frac{1}{3} - 2 =$ | $5\frac{1}{3}$ |
| **L** | $2\frac{1}{2} \times 2\frac{2}{3} =$ | $6\frac{2}{3}$ |
| **N** | $9\frac{3}{4} - 4\frac{1}{2} =$ | $5\frac{1}{4}$ |
| **D** | $2\frac{2}{3} + 1\frac{2}{3} =$ | $4\frac{1}{3}$ |
| **C** | $\frac{1}{3} + \frac{1}{3} =$ | $\frac{2}{3}$ |

$\underset{4\frac{5}{6}}{S}\ \underset{\frac{1}{4}}{O}\ \underset{5\frac{3}{4}}{M}\ \underset{1\frac{4}{5}}{E}\ \underset{\frac{1}{4}}{O}\ \underset{5\frac{1}{4}}{N}\ \underset{1\frac{4}{5}}{E}$

$\underset{4\frac{5}{6}}{S}\ \underset{1\frac{5}{12}}{T}\ \underset{\frac{1}{4}}{O}\ \underset{6\frac{2}{3}}{L}\ \underset{1\frac{4}{5}}{E}$

$\underset{4\frac{5}{6}}{S}\ \underset{1\frac{4}{5}}{E}\ \underset{\frac{2}{3}}{C}\ \underset{\frac{1}{4}}{O}\ \underset{5\frac{1}{4}}{N}\ \underset{4\frac{1}{3}}{D}$

$\underset{2}{B}\ \underset{5\frac{1}{3}}{A}\ \underset{4\frac{5}{6}}{S}\ \underset{1\frac{4}{5}}{E}$

## Page 58

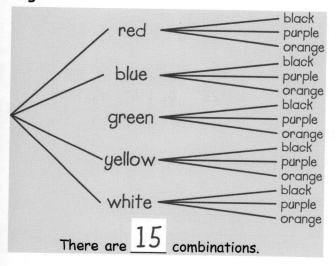

There are **15** combinations.

## Page 59

Factor tree will vary, but the last row for each factor tree should be:

1. 3 × 5
2. 2 × 2 × 2 × 3
3. 2 × 2 × 2 × 2 × 2
4. 2 × 7
5. 3 × 3 × 5
6. 2 × 2 × 2 × 5
7. 5 × 5
8. 2 × 2 × 2 × 2 × 5
9. 2 × 2 × 2 × 2

## Page 60

1. 1,040 feet
2. 57,600 square feet

## Page 61

From top to bottom:

10. 27
9. 55
8. 5
7. 14
6. 22
5. 23
4. 5
3. 10
2. 2
1. 135

## Page 62

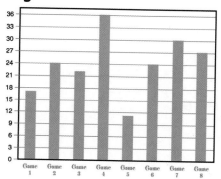

## Page 63

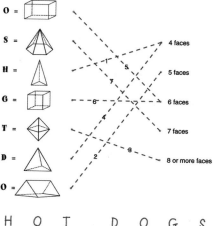

$\underset{1}{H}\ \underset{2}{O}\ \underset{3}{T}\quad \underset{4}{D}\ \underset{5}{O}\ \underset{6}{G}\ \underset{7}{S}$

## Page 64

1. C     7. C    12.
2. D     8. D
3. A     9. B
4. C    10. B
5. A    11. D
6. D

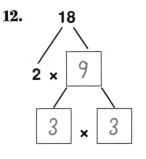

## Unit 6

## Page 65

1. ray; $\overrightarrow{XY}$

2. line; $\overleftrightarrow{QR}$

3. perpendicular lines; $\overleftrightarrow{JK} \perp \overleftrightarrow{MN}$

4. parallel lines; $\overleftrightarrow{GH} \parallel \overleftrightarrow{YZ}$

## Page 66

1. Draw a line segment. Label it AB.

3. Draw a ray. Label it DE.

2. Draw parallel lines. Label the lines MN and PR.

4. Draw perpendicular lines. Label the lines WX and YZ.

## Page 67

1. acute    5. obtuse
2. obtuse   6. acute
3. obtuse   7. right
4. obtuse   8. acute

## Page 68

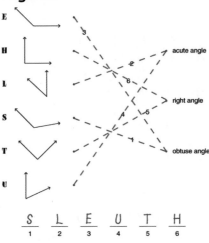

$\underset{1}{S} \quad \underset{2}{L} \quad \underset{3}{E} \quad \underset{4}{U} \quad \underset{5}{T} \quad \underset{6}{H}$

## Page 69

1. 90°    3. 75°    5. 45°    7. 55°
2. 135°   4. 125°   6. 145°   8. 140°

## Page 70

A RIGHT ANGLE

## Page 71

| Figure | Number of Faces | Number of Edges | Number of Vertices |
|---|---|---|---|
| edge → face, vertex | 6 | 12 | 8 |
| | 6 | 12 | 8 |
| | 5 | 9 | 6 |
| | 5 | 8 | 5 |
| | 7 | 12 | 7 |

## Page 72

SIX SMALL SLICK SEALS

Math • EMC 4550 • ©2005 by Evan-Moor Corp.

## Page 73

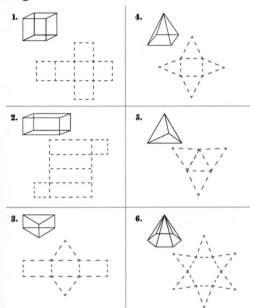

## Page 74

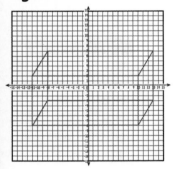

## Page 75

1. cylinder
2. cone
3. rectangular prism
4. sphere
5. pyramid

## Page 76

1. congruent
2. similar
3. congruent
4. similar
5. similar
6. congruent

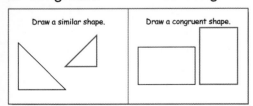

## Page 77

1. D
2. A
3. C
4. B
5. A
6. C
7. B
8. Child should draw an angle that measures 45°.
9. A
10. D
11. B
12.

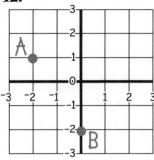

### Unit 7

## Page 78

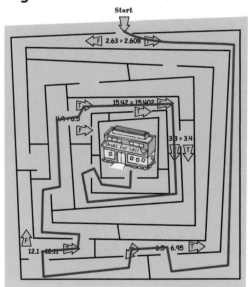

## Page 79

1. 3
2. 25
3. 14
4. 150
5. 1.5
6. 12.5
7. 7
8. 75
9. 2.4
10. 20
11. 11.2
12. 120
13. 4.5
14. 37.5
15. 21
16. 225

## Page 80

1. $38
2. $15
3. 0.4; $21.60
4. $16; $17
5. 0.065

## Page 81

1. 166 feet
2. Yes. If you make the shape a rectangle with the dimensions 28 feet by 55 feet, you can use the formula for perimeter, $P = 2 \times \text{length} \times 2 \times \text{width}$.

## Page 82

1.

| Size | Color |
|--------|--------|
| small | blue |
| small | yellow |
| medium | blue |
| medium | yellow |
| large | blue |
| large | yellow |

2.

| Design | Color |
|-----------|--------|
| striped | red |
| striped | purple |
| striped | orange |
| polka-dots | red |
| polka-dots | purple |
| polka-dots | orange |
| checkered | red |
| checkered | purple |
| checkered | orange |

## Page 83

A LCM of 2 and 4 = 4
E LCM of 5 and 6 = 30
E LCM of 3 and 4 = 12
E LCM of 4 and 5 = 20
E LCM of 6 and 9 = 18
S LCM of 5 and 3 = 15

T LCM of 7 and 3 = 21
T LCM of 22 and 4 = 44
T LCM of 16 and 3 = 48
W LCM of 6 and 8 = 24
W LCM of 10 and 8 = 40

$\underset{4}{A}$ $\underset{15}{S}$ $\underset{40}{W}$ $\underset{12}{E}$ $\underset{30}{E}$ $\underset{44}{T}$

$\underset{21}{T}$ $\underset{24}{W}$ $\underset{20}{E}$ $\underset{18}{E}$ $\underset{48}{T}$

## Page 84

S $2\frac{1}{4} + 3\frac{1}{2} = 5\frac{3}{4}$
H $2\frac{2}{3} + 1\frac{2}{3} = 4\frac{1}{3}$
O $8\frac{3}{4} - 3\frac{1}{2} = 5\frac{1}{4}$
E $7\frac{1}{3} - 2 = 5\frac{1}{3}$

S $2\frac{1}{4} + 3\frac{2}{2} = 5\frac{3}{4}$
H $2\frac{7}{12} + 1\frac{3}{4} = 4\frac{1}{3}$
O $9\frac{3}{4} - 4\frac{1}{2} = 5\frac{1}{4}$
P $6\frac{1}{3} - 1\frac{5}{6} = 4\frac{1}{2}$

## Page 85

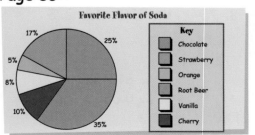

Favorite Flavor of Soda

1. 35%
2. 30%
3. 100%

## Page 86

1. $56.25 < $63.00
2. $24 > $18
3. Jan and Max; $68 = $68

## Page 87

1. $47.45; $12.55
2. $27.95
3. $1.57; $15.70
4. $8.45
5. $11.74

## Page 88

Alicia went to the Shoe Store.
Ann went to the Book Store.
Geraldo went to the Games Store.
Rachel went to the Pet Shop.
Raul went to the Video Store.
Tim went to the Sandwich Nook.

## Page 89

1. C
2. D
3. A
4. $18\frac{7}{12}$
5. B
6. D
7. C
8. C
9. A
10. D

11.

| Shirt | Pants |
|-------|-------|
| red | blue |
| red | black |
| blue | blue |
| blue | black |
| green | blue |
| green | black |

12. C

## Page 90

1. 1
2. 4
3. 0
4. 9
5. 15
6. 13
7. 17
8. 22
9. 31
10. 4
11. 6
12. 6
13. 4
14. 11
15. 14
16. 27
17. 7
18. 48

Math • EMC 4550 • ©2005 by Evan-Moor Corp.

## Page 91

1. 16
2. 8
3. 243
4. 64
5. 1,024
6. 125
7. 31
8. 235
9. 675
10. 3

## Page 92

1. 40
2. 24
3. 30
4. 20.4
5. 28
6. 21
7. 31.4
8. 27.1
9. $29\frac{1}{3}$
10. 32

## Page 93

| Shape | Formula | Perimeter |
|---|---|---|
| square, 3 | P = 4 × s | P = 4 × _3_<br>P = _12_ |
| rectangle, 5, 3 | P = (2 × w) + (2 × l) | P = (2 × _3_) + (2 × _5_)<br>P = _6_ + _10_<br>P = _16_ |
| rhombus, 5 | P = 4 × s | P = 4 × _5_<br>P = _20_ |
| parallelogram, 8, 4 | P = (2 × w) + (2 × l) | P = (2 × _4_) + (2 × _8_)<br>P = _8_ + _16_<br>P = _24_ |
| equilateral triangle, 5 | P = 3 × s | P = 3 × _5_<br>P = _15_ |

## Page 94

1. 42
2. 16
3. 24
4. 20
5. 60
6. 16
7. 225
8. 162
9. 441
10. 54

## Page 95

Trapezoid 1: 15 square inches
Trapezoid 2: 26 square inches
Trapezoid 3: 75 square inches

## Page 96

| Shape | Formula | Area |
|---|---|---|
| square, 4 | $A = s^2$ | A = _4_ × _4_<br>A = _16_ square units |
| rectangle, 6, 4 | A = b × h | A = _6_ × _4_<br>A = _24_ square units |
| rhombus, 6 | A = b × h | A = _6_ × _6_<br>A = _36_ square units |
| parallelogram, 5.5, 7.5 | A = b × h | A = _7.5_ × _5.5_<br>A = _41.25_ square units |
| equilateral triangle, 3, 4 | $A = \frac{b \times h}{2}$ | A = $\frac{\boxed{4} \times \boxed{3}}{2}$<br>A = _6_ square units |

## Page 97

1. 45
2. 140
3. 8
4. 420
5. 512
6. 360

## Page 98

1. The perimeters are the same.
   6 + 6 + 6 + 6 = 24 and
   4 + 4 + 4 + 4 + 4 + 4 = 24
2. Shape B has a larger area because
   12 > 10.
3. Box B has a larger volume because
   343 > 315.

## Page 99

1. 28.26 in.²
2. 50.24 in.²
3. 113.04 cm²
4. 153.86 cm²
5. 254.34 in.²
6. 314 in.²
7. 12.56 cm²
8. 78.5 in.²
9. 200.96 cm²
10. 63.585 in.²

## Page 100

A FLAG

## Page 101

1. 50.24
2. 25.12
3. 12.56
4. 37.68
5. 62.8
6. 69.08
7. 43.96
8. 18.84
9. 56.52
10. 43.96
11. 31.4
12. 31.4

©2005 by Evan-Moor Corp. • EMC 4550 • Math

## Page 102

| | | | | | | | |
|---|---|---|---|---|---|---|---|
| **1.** D | **4.** B | **7.** D | **10.** A |
| **2.** B | **5.** D | **8.** A | **11.** B |
| **3.** D | **6.** C | **9.** B | **12.** A |

## Unit 9

## Page 103

H  ⁻6 + ⁺9 =  $+3$

L  ⁺9 + ⁻2 =  $+7$

L  ⁻3 + ⁻12 =  $^-15$

N  ⁻4 + ⁻8 =  $^-12$

O  ⁺7 + ⁻7 =  $0$

O  ⁻6 + ⁻4 =  $^-10$

U  ⁻8 + ⁺2 =  $^-6$

U  ⁺11 + ⁻6 =  $+5$

| H | O | N | O | L | U | L | U |
|---|---|---|---|---|---|---|---|
| +3 | ⁻10 | ⁻12 | 0 | +7 | ⁻6 | ⁻15 | +5 |

## Page 104

PU A      ALOALO

0  1  2  3  4  5  6  7  8  9  10  11  12  13

## Page 105

1. Lanai, Molokai, Kauai, Oahu, Maui, Hawai'i
2. Hawai'i, Oahu, Maui, Kauai, Molokai, Lanai
3. No; there is no relationship between the area and the coastlines of the islands.

## Page 106

1. $1,437.00
2. Yes, she saved $1,500 and spent $1,437.

## Page 107

**1.** Rule = +2.45

| Input | Output |
|---|---|
| 3 | 5.45 |
| 2.1 | 4.55 |
| 4.16 | 6.61 |
| 2.75 | 5.2 |

**2.** Rule = −3.25

| Input | Output |
|---|---|
| 5 | 1.75 |
| 6.19 | 2.94 |
| 7.4 | 4.15 |
| 6.75 | 3.5 |

**3.** Rule = +1 −3

| Input | Output |
|---|---|
| 5 | 3 |
| 13 | 11 |
| 19 | 17 |
| 22 | 20 |

**4.** Rule = ×2 +1½

| Input | Output |
|---|---|
| 5 | 11½ |
| 1½ | 4½ |
| 3¼ | 8 |
| 0 | 1½ |

**5.** Rule = ÷2 +1

| Input | Output |
|---|---|
| 8 | 5 |
| 12 | 7 |
| 15 | 8.5 |
| 29 | 15.5 |

**6.** Rule = ×3.2 +4.9

| Input | Output |
|---|---|
| 1.2 | 8.74 |
| 0.8 | 7.46 |
| 2 | 11.3 |
| 1.6 | 10.02 |

**7.** Rule = ÷2 +6.41

| Input | Output |
|---|---|
| 4 | 8.41 |
| 5 | 8.91 |
| 8 | 10.41 |
| 11 | 11.91 |

**8.** Rule = ×⅓ +¼

| Input | Output |
|---|---|
| 3 | 1¼ |
| 6 | 2¼ |
| 9 | 3¼ |
| 12 | 4¼ |

**9.** Rule = ×½ +½

| Input | Output |
|---|---|
| 8 | 4½ |
| 9 | 5 |
| 13 | 7 |
| 16 | 8½ |

## Page 108

A  What is the percent form of ½?  50%

B  What is the fraction form of 30%?  3/10

D  What is the decimal form of 40%?  0.4

E  What is the fraction form of 80%?  8/10

G  What is the fraction form of 75%?  3/4

H  What is the fraction form of 0.25?  1/4

I  What is the decimal form of 43%?  0.43

I  What is the fraction form of 40%?  2/5

L  What is the decimal form of 80%?  0.8

N  What is the percent form of 0.9?  90%

S  What is the percent form of 0.09?  9%

T  What is the decimal form of ½?  0.5

| T | H | E | | B | I | G |
|---|---|---|---|---|---|---|
| 0.5 | ¼ | 8/10 | | 3/10 | ⅖ | ¾ |

| I | S | L | A | N | D |
|---|---|---|---|---|---|
| 0.43 | 9% | 0.8 | 50% | 90% | 0.4 |

## Page 109

1. $1,389.32
2. $1,238.82
3. $619.41
4. 26 weeks

Math • EMC 4550 • ©2005 by Evan-Moor Corp.

## Page 110

A What is the LCM of 1 and 5? _5_  
D What is the LCM of 2 and 3? _6_  
E What is the LCM of 3 and 9? _9_  
F What is the LCM of 1 and 11? _11_  
H What is the LCM of 16 and 2? _16_  
N What is the LCM of 17 and 1? _17_  
O What is the LCM of 13 and 1? _13_  

R What is the LCM of 18 and 3? _18_  
S What is the LCM of 14 and 2? _14_  
T What is the LCM of 3 and 5? _15_  
U What is the LCM of 1 and 7? _7_  
W What is the LCM of 2 and 5? _10_  
Y What is the LCM of 8 and 2? _8_  

T W E N T Y - F O U R  
15 10 9 17 15 8   11 13 7 18  

T H O U S A N D  
15 16 13 7 14 5 17 6  

## Page 111

1. No, their total weight would be 508 pounds which is more than the 500 pound limit.
2. 24 ounces or 1 pound 8 ounces or 1½ pounds
3. $\frac{3}{8}$ full
4. 6,370 feet

## Page 112

Any 4 of the following 8 possible trails:
1. Valley Trail, Mountain Trail, Cliff Trail
2. Valley Trail, Mountain Trail, High Trail, Steep Trail
3. Valley Trail, River Trail, High Trail, Cliff Trail
4. Valley Trail, River Trail, Steep Trail
5. Blue Trail, River Trail, Mountain Trail, Cliff Trail
6. Blue Trail, River Trail, Mountain Trail, High Trail, Steep Trail
7. Blue Trail, High Trail, Cliff Trail
8. Blue Trail, Steep Trail

## Page 113

Adams family went hiking.  
Chen family went fishing.  
Hernandes family went kayaking.  
Jordan family went scuba diving.  
Probst family went surfing.  
Rice family went bicycling.

## Page 114

1. C
2. D
3. B
4. D
5. B
6. C
7. D
8. C
9. B
10. A
11. D
12. A

## Unit 10

## Page 115

G A S  
36 64 81  

G I A N T S  
27 125 64 25 32 49  

A $4^3$ = _64_  
A $8^2$ = _64_  
G $6^2$ = _36_  
G $3^3$ = _27_  
I $5^3$ = _125_  
N $5^2$ = _25_  
S $9^2$ = _81_  
S $7^2$ = _49_  
T $2^5$ = _32_  

## Page 116

C O N S T E L L A T I O N S

Fill in the circle in front of the meaning of the mystery word.

● the name for groups of planets orbiting a sun

○ a body in space with a solid mass and a tail of gas and dust

○ various groups of stars that have been given names

## Page 117

1. (−5, 6)
2. comet W; star Y
3. (6, −5)
4.

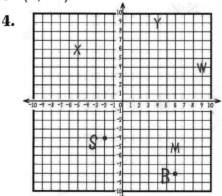

## Page 118

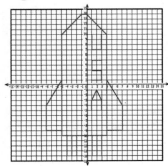

## Page 119

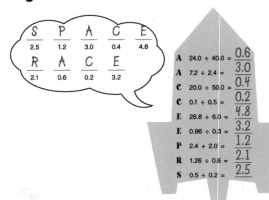

S P A C E
2.5  1.2  3.0  0.4  4.8

R A C E
2.1  0.6  0.2  3.2

A  24.0 ÷ 40.0 = $\underline{0.6}$
A  7.2 ÷ 2.4 = $\underline{3.0}$
C  20.0 ÷ 50.0 = $\underline{0.4}$
C  0.1 ÷ 0.5 = $\underline{0.2}$
E  28.8 ÷ 6.0 = $\underline{4.8}$
E  0.96 ÷ 0.3 = $\underline{3.2}$
P  2.4 ÷ 2.0 = $\underline{1.2}$
R  1.26 ÷ 0.6 = $\underline{2.1}$
S  0.5 ÷ 0.2 = $\underline{2.5}$

## Page 120

1. 300
2. 49,000
3. 27,540
4. 180,000
5. 300,000
6. 1,700,000
7. 6,000,000
8. 7,500,000
9. 3,000,000
10. 15,000,000

## Page 121

1. 4,879.91 km
2. 12,108.81 km
3. 12,760.86 km
4. 6,797.42 km
5. 142,853.69 km
6. 120,106 km
7. 52,486 km
8. 48,622 km

## Page 122

| | Set of Data | Range | Mean | Median | Mode |
|---|---|---|---|---|---|
| 1. | 15, 23, 23, 24, 26 | 11 | 22.2 | 23 | 23 |
| 2. | 1, 2, 4, 4, 4, 5, 8, 9 | 8 | 4.625 | 4 | 4 |
| 3. | 6, 6, 6, 6, 6, 6, 6, | 0 | 6 | 6 | 6 |
| 4. | 21, 23, 25, 28, 32, 39 | 18 | 28 | 26.5 | none |
| 5. | 40, 45, 50, 55, 60, 65, 70 | 30 | 55 | 55 | none |

## Page 123

$^-5 - {}^+2 = \underline{-7}$

$^-2 - {}^-3 = \underline{+1}$

$^-10 - {}^-6 = \underline{-4}$

$^-7 - {}^+3 = \underline{-10}$

$^+2 - {}^-7 = \underline{+9}$

$^-2 - {}^+4 = \underline{-6}$

$^-8 - {}^-7 = \underline{-1}$

## Page 124

THE MILKY WAY

## Page 125

1. Translate to the right.

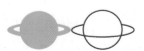

2. Rotate to the left 90 degrees.

3. Reflect across the dashed line.

4. Translate to the right.

5. Reflect across the dashed line.